HISPANIC ELDERLY:

A Cultural Signature

Marta Sotomayor, Editor
Herman Curiel, Co-Editor

A Publication of the
National Hispanic Council on Aging

Pan American University Press
Edinburg, TX 78539
1988

Library of Congress Cataloging-in-Publication Data

Hispanic elderly

"A publication of the National Hispanic Council on Aging".

1. Hispanic American aged.   I. Sotomayor, Marta.
II. Curiel, Herman. III. National Hispanic Council on Aging (U.S.)
HQ1064.U5H53 1988
ISBN: 0-938738-07-0

Cover design by Frank R. Manuella
Book design by Patricia De La Fuente

PAN AMERICAN UNIVERSITY
1201 W. University Drive / Edinburg, TX 78539-2999

HISPANIC ELDERLY:

A Cultural Signature

Preface

As in all complex research and writing endeavors, this book is the product of many individuals whose names do not necessarily appear in it: the research site coordinators, the interviewers, and the students. I would, however, like to mention several people without whose support the production of this important book would have not been possible.

First, I would like to acknowledge the advice and consultation provided by Dr. Juan Ramón Valle, California State University at San Diego, who assisted us in the initial conceptualization of the research project. Very special thanks must be given to Dr. Alvin O. Korte, New Mexico Highlands University, who did at least 80 percent of the work required to carry out the research task. His appreciation for research, the actual joy of discovery and satisfaction in confirming what we at times might label "intuition," encouraged him to go on despite the many barriers encountered in a project of this size and the limited resources available to carry it out.

Special thanks are given to Dr. Delores Reed-Sanders, Pan American University, without whom this book might not have been written. Her leadership, initiative, patience, and resourcefulness are greatly appreciated. Thanks are also given to each of the writers who contributed to the production of this book and who did so despite the limited time that they were given to complete this task and despite my "as soon as possible" demands. Yet, they completed this task with precision, punctuality, and pride. They did so knowing the importance of this document to the well-being of our Hispanic elderly and their commitment to improve it.

Beyond acknowledgment of the work that each of the contributors spent on the completion of this project, I would like to acknowledge the participation of our Hispanic elderly who answered our questions that oftentimes seemed impertinent and out of order. With much respect, admiration, and affection, this work is dedicated to them as we continue our efforts to make their life more bearable.

This research project was supported by the Administration on Aging, Office of Human Development, Department of Health and Human Services, Washington, D.C.

Marta Sotomayor, President
National Hispanic Council on Aging
Washington D.C.
April 7, 1988

TABLE OF CONTENTS

PART II : Theoretical and Methodological Implications of the Cultural Context of Coping

PART III : Socio-Economic Implications on the Well-Being of Hispanic Elderly

PART IV : Conclusions and Recommendations

The Hispanic Elderly:
A Cultural Signature
Introduction

Marta Sotomayor

Low utilization rates of human and health care services by the Hispanic elderly have become so severe that this is regarded as a significant social policy issue by Hispanic gerontologists. Problems related to this issue will become even more complex given the projected growth of Hispanics, a group which now constitutes the nation's second largest minority. Yet, we know very little about the various Hispanic sub-population groups due to the dearth of systematic, on-going research about the various aspects of their life experiences. The understanding of differences based on ethnic, racial, cultural, and linguistic variations that determine how people view themselves, relate to one another, and solve problems has been recognized as a prerequisite to the development of effective service delivery systems that are meaningful and acceptable.

In general, information included herein is of considerable signifi-cance in view of the gaps in knowledge about this growing and varied population group. These articles address important considerations within a cultural perspective that will increase the understanding of at least two groups of Hispanic elderly, Mexican-Americans and Puerto Ricans.

The Research Project:

We initially sought to explore the events and interpersonal relationships among the various layers of the Hispanic intergenerational family
that could influence the coping styles of the elderly. But, the points of
stress, or "markers", in the life cycle of the intergenerational family, as
precipitated and/or caused by other structures and socio-political forces
outside the family unit, often surfaced as topics to be explored.

While a key interest of the planners of this research project was
the identification and examination of the various patterns, styles, and/or
coping skills characteristic of or preferred by the Hispanic elderly, the
over-all goal was to increase the understanding of the multiple-layer
phenomena that comprise the development of appropriate and
meaningful services for this particular group of elderly.

Lack of Access and Low Utilization Rates of Services:

Neither the factors that determine the access to and utilization of
existing services by the Hispanic elderly nor the various meanings of
cultural/linguistic services have yet been systematically examined over
periods of time. However, the literature on the subject suggests the
following explanations:

1. the Hispanic elderly go without needed services because of
   inadequacies of the formal helping systems;
2. other forms of indigenous helping structures and modalities
   are preferred by them; thus, the need for formal services is
   diminished;
3. factors associated with social and economic status, prejudice,
   discrimination, and/or cultural insensitivity on the part of

          service providers contribute to the low service utilization rates.

It is not clear how these factors interact with one another. For example, the less need can be explained in terms of family-sharing resources and the use of indigenous helping modalities. Discriminatory institutional policies overlap with the irrelevancy of existing services; and still one could be the result of the other. Answers to these key questions are forthcoming only if we commit ourselves to conduct longitudinal and comparative studies with sub-population groups of Hispanics dispersed in different geographical areas of the country. As an initial step, this work examines a number of areas that may add to the understanding of these multiple and complex factors.

The Cultural Context of Coping:

          Coping is inextricably related to the quality of one's life experiences, for the ability and the skills one has, chooses, or is able to use to cope determine how life's strains and stresses are handled so that their painful or paralyzing effects can be avoided, prevented, or controlled. As such, coping can be related not only to personal resources, but also to particular life styles and environmental resources available to deal with life. According to this perspective, individuals can either respond to stresses with their own personal resources or with coping resources. Personal resources consist of strengths a person has, such as life experience, cognitive and perceptual skills and how these are used in relation to others and themselves. Coping responses can be viewed as those behaviors that are used when actually contending with life's problems. They represent things that people do in dealing with life's events and stresses. Both individual and group behaviors, what people do, or can do, are to a significant degree determined by one's cultural world view and life experience.

Coping responses can be categorized into distinguishable areas according to their function and the context within which they occur. For example, coping responses can produce change in situations that are stress-producing experiences, or they can control the meaning of such experiences after they occur to prevent dysfunction stress, or actually control stress itself after it has emerged. The use of one function or the other can also be influenced by specific life experiences or perceptions present at different stages in the life cycle of individuals and groups.

The Research Instrument:

An initial goal of the research project was to develop a data collection instrument that would examine and identify variables associated with coping characteristics of two Hispanic sub-groups of elderly. After reviewing a variety of research instruments with a panel of research consultants, a decision was made to develop an instrument using variations and/or portions of several scales that would yield information on the following areas:

1. a description and the causes of stress situations encountered by the elderly in the process of daily living;
2. indicators of self-esteem, mastery, and perceptions of health status.

The questionnaire included:

1. a four item self-denigration scale;
2. a five item self-esteem scale;
3. an eight item assimilation scale;
4. a seven item mastery scale;
5. a five item help-received scale;

6. a six item help-giving scale; and

7. a thirteen item life-satisfaction scale.

The combined instrument allowed for the study of 275 variables that took an average of two hours to administer.

The Research Methodology:

The data for the articles presented in this book were gathered via in-person interviews with low-income Mexican-American and Puerto Rican respondents 65 years old or older. The sample design used four sites to produce a multi-stage area sample. Two primary urban areas located in different parts of the country were selected: Hartford, CT. and San Antonio, TX. Two primarily rural sites were also selected: The Rio Grande Valley of Texas and Northern New Mexico. Criteria for inclusion in the study included five years or more residence in the United States, lack of an incapacitating physical ailment, and willingness to participate in the study.

Sampling units in the urban areas were primary sampling units (PSU) of the U.S. Bureau of the Census. Enumeration districts were used as the primary sampling units for the rural areas. The enumeration districts were selected at random and within that enumeration district, only one area was selected for inclusion. One-half of the respondents were thus selected as a "community sample". The other half of the respondents were selected from households known to social service agencies such as *El Centro del Barrio* in San Antonio, Texas, and *Casa de Amigos* in McAllen, Texas. These clients were listed and then a random selection was made from that list. Thus, while the sample is not truly a random sample, there are various aspects of randomness built into the design. The study design had households as the unit of analysis and in 44 households conjoint interviewees were used. The articles included

in this book do not make use of data obtained in those conjoint interviews. The decision to delete the data obtained in conjoint interviews
was based on a concern that some scale items were jointly coded, risking
a possible invalidation of the item. Thus, this conservative approach is
restricted to the remaining 347 completed interviews which were individually administered.

The Chapters:

The articles included in this book are by no means a complete
representation of the data collected. Some of the chapters focus on a
specific aspect, style, or factor that influences coping such as mastery,
self-esteem, life-satisfaction, and levels of acculturation. One article
discusses traditional assumptions about familism based on data collected; perceptions of health status, family caregiving issues, and
religiosity are also addressed. Methodological issues are mentioned in
another article, particularly as they refer to the applicability of the scales
to measuring the life experiences of these two groups of elderly.

While each of the articles included in this volume reflect the
specific research interest of the authors, as a whole they address key
research issues that will add to the understanding of the cultural variables
that influence functional coping styles used by Hispanic elderly. Further
pursuit of this line of inquiry depends on those who may be encouraged
by these articles to undertake additional research in the area. In many
respects this is an initial effort. The Hispanic elderly experience should
continue to be examined from many perspectives, using a wide variety of
data sources and methodological approaches. What is of most
importance is that we continue to build our knowledge base and thus
increase the understanding of this particular life experience. To this end,
this book is a contribution to the field of gerontology and a way to solidify

the cross-cultural, linguistic, and the often troublesome socio-political relationships that characterize the Hispanic experience.

In this text the authors use the term Hispanic to mean Latino, Mexican-American, Chicano, Hispano, and Puerto Rican. The subjects in this study were primarily of Mexican heritage with the exception of subjects in Hartford, Connecticut, who self-identified as Puerto Rican.

PART I:

The Cultural Context of Coping

The Influence of Aging on Self-Esteem: A Consideration of Ethnicity, Gender, and Acculturation Level Differences

Herman Curiel and James A. Rosenthal

The physical, psychological, and social changes that accompany advancing age require continued adjustments that tax the adaptive resources of the older person. How one builds internal strengths, develops more self-awareness, learns new ways of coping with oftentimes cumulative losses, and seeks meaning from living has a lot to do with one's attitudes, belief systems, and previous ways of adjusting to loss (Beaver & Miller, 1985). Members of ethnic minority groups who have struggled to keep their belief systems alive in an environment that rewards change experience additional challenges. The situation of elderly individuals who are members of identifiable ethnic minority populations has been characterized by minority group advocates as that of "double jeopardy" or "multiple hazards" (Jackson, 1970). These descriptions refer to the additive effects of being old and subject to additional economic, social, and psychological burdens of living in a society in which racial equality remains more myth than social policy (Bengtson, 1979). Demographic characteristics of Hispanic elderly compiled by the U.S. Census

Bureau (1987) suggest that in terms of relative income, level of formal education, employment history, and health status Hispanic elderly may indeed be characterized as experiencing "multiple hazards."

How one maintains one's sense of self-worth or self-esteem is an important consideration in maintaining good mental health. Burns (1979) defines self-esteem as the process by which individuals examine their performance, capacities, and attributes according to their personal standards and values, which have been internalized from interactions with society and significant others. In minority groups the family acts as a source of nurturance and protection to offset messages from the dominant societal group that define "a minority person's" difference as negative and a threat to the values of the majority culture. The elder person's role in the family is changing as more Hispanics adopt the nuclear family model (Maldonado, 1975). A number of scholars have noted a relationship between loss of social roles in the aged and the effects of this loss on self-esteem. The importance of feeling useful and needed for the maintenance of a sense of worth and self-esteem is a crucial issue addressed in a number of social programs (Korte, 1980).

The focus of this study is on Hispanic elderly. Hispanics in the United States represent a number of subgroups who share similar values, a mother language, traditions and customs that are a mixture of Spanish, Indian, African, and possess varying degrees of assimilation to the American culture which is heavily influenced by White Anglo-Saxon Protestant values. Hispanic adults 65 years and over represent 4.9 percent of the total Hispanic population, or 906,000 persons (Cubillos, 1987). Mexican-Americans comprise a majority of Hispanic elderly population at 54.1 percent (491,000). Cubans represent 13.6 percent (123,000), Puerto Ricans 8.9 percent (81,000), Central and South Americans 6.5 percent (59,000) and other Hispanics represent 16.6 percent (151,000). Other Hispanics represent persons primarily from New Mexico who designate themselves as Hispanic or Hispanos (Bureau of Census, 1987).

These groups' ethnic identification is influenced by their respective country of origin experience, length of residence or history of family in the United States, and the cumulative experience of interactions with members of the majority and other minority groups. Korte (1980) says the effect that historical events such as migration, acculturation, urbanization, and discrimination have on ethnic consciousness can be understood as both subjective (a sense of personal identity) and as an awareness of the social order to which one is a part. Belonging to a community of people whose traditional values are shared becomes increasingly significant or meaningful as individuals age. Ethnic identification is defined as a common awareness with persons of same origin. This awareness represents a subset of group identification that deals with the perception of sharing common interests in a variety of contexts such as professions, generational groupings, or religious affiliation. A sense of ethnicity affects the maintenance of cultural traditions, helps organize a social structure, offers opportunities for mobility and success, and allows individuals the opportunity to enhance their self-concept in a large, impersonal society (García, 1982).

An important role of culture is that of prescribing gender roles. The Hispanic culture is a culture that dramatically restricts the range of male and female behaviors. The Mexican family, a subset of Hispanic families, is purportedly founded on the supremacy of the father and the corresponding total self-sacrifice of the mother (Díaz-Guerrero, 1955). More recent studies of Hispanic families have challenged the popular accepted notion of absolute and unbending male dominance (Cromwell & Ruiz, 1979; Baca-Zinn, 1980). Women's roles in the majority culture are becoming more fluid. Such changes influence women's roles in minority groups and are producing changes in traditionally Hispanic held beliefs of sex roles. How elderly Hispanic males and females adapt to the changing role of women in the larger society is an important question for mental health professionals. The loss of the traditional Hispanic male role introduces a dilemma for both sexes, and particularly for the male who may begin to doubt his sense of worth and importance in the family. Add to this the loss of the bread-winner role and the possibility of having to supplement the family income with public funds further erodes the elderly Hispanic male's self-esteem.

To be or not to be part of the majority culture is a dilemma for members of ethnic minority groups. Is it possible to have an identity that incorporates the best of the majority and minority cultures? How one resolves these questions has consequences for later years when a person's resources become more limited.

Acculturation is an adaptive process of cultural adjustment that takes individuals through several different phases changing their conditions of life. The acculturative process begins as a result of contact and interaction between two or more autonomous cultural groups (Mena, Padilla, & Maldonado, 1987). Hispanic culture has been found to differ considerably from the dominant Anglo-American culture with regard to numerous psychological dimensions. Furthermore, the United States Hispanic population contains a wide range

of intragroup variability with regard to country of origin and the extent
to which individuals have adopted the sociocultural and psychological characteristics of the host society (Burnam et al., 1987).
Previous research has identified individual characteristics which may
promote or inhibit changes in level of acculturation. Several studies
have found a relationship between level of acculturation and age
among Hispanic Americans (Ibid., 1987). The melting pot and
bicultural hypotheses indicate opposite predictions regarding the
relationship between acculturation and psychological adjustment.
The melting pot hypothesis predicts that the more acculturated the
Hispanic is, the less the occurrence of psychological problems. The
opposite view, the bicultural hypothesis, holds that the Hispanic who
is acculturated, but maintains a footing in the traditional culture is
more adaptive than the completely acculturated Hispanic (Griffith,
1983). Studies by Buriel et al. (1982) and Szapocznik et al. (1980)
support the bicultural hypothesis.

Purpose

The purpose of this investigation is to examine the relationship
of self-esteem with level of acculturation, ethnic identification, gender,
and type of support system. For purposes of this study, two groups
were identified. The "agency" group is distinguished from the
"community" group on the basis of type of support system used. The
"agency" subjects had a formal relationship with a careprovider
institution. The "community" group's functioning did not require a
formal support system. It is assumed that the latter group used
informal support systems, such as family, neighbors, or friends. It is
expected that Hispanic elderly who are functioning with the support of

an informal network will perceive themselves more positively than those requiring a more formal support system. It is further hypothesized that Hispanic females compared to Hispanic males in either "agency" or "community" group will perceive themselves more positively. It is also hypothesized that a positive correlation between subjects' self-esteem and acculturation level scores will be found. And finally, it is hypothesized that subjects of Mexican ancestry will perceive themselves more positively than their Puerto Rican counterparts because of their greater number of years in this country.

Survey of Literature

Literature on minority aging is growing, but it is still sparse on the Hispanic elderly. In a survey of published research, Becerra & Shaw (1984) indicate that the available works suggest that ethnicity, cultural characteristics, and socioeconomic status are related both to the physical health and to the psychic well-being of Hispanic elders.

Much of the research in the area of ethnicity and mental health has approached the subject matter from the "social stress" or "social causation" perspective commonly evoked to account for greater psychopathology among lower social classes (Markides & Mendel, 1987).

Research conducted by Vega (1980) and Meinhart & Vega (1982) using four measures of psychiatric distress identified certain subgroups of Hispanics as especially vulnerable. These subgroups include the more monolingual (Spanish-speaking only), the Mexican-American middle-aged woman (40-59), and older males (60-69 years). These two groups were found to have unusually high levels of stress, health, and mental health dysfunction. The literature suggests that Hispanics are subject to greater health and mental health dysfunction due to tensions and stresses related to their minority status (Karno & Edgerton, 1969; Torres-Gil, 1978; Cervantes & Castro, 1985).

Self-esteem and self-concept are frequently treated as being synonymous in the literature on self-evaluation. Self-esteem refers to a basic feeling of self-worth, a belief that one is fundamentally a person of value. George (1987) distinguishes the two concepts; she views self-concept as the cognitive component of the self that consists of the individual's perceptions of him/herself as an object (i.e. what I am really like). Self-esteem, on the other hand, she says, refers to affective judgments emerging from individuals' comparisons of what they are like to what they aspire to be like.

In the psychology literature, self-esteem is viewed as an important component of individual personality which influences a person's mental health or intrapsychic well-being (see works of Alfred Adler, Gordon W. Alport, Abraham H. Maslow, Carl R.Rogers). In the field of sociology, the role theory of P. Secord and J. G. Backman and the symbolic interactionists perspectives of C. H. Cooley, G. H. Mead, and H. W. Kuhn have given considerable attention to self-esteem. These sociological perspectives emphasize the critical role of social interaction and significant others in the development and mainte-nance of self-esteem (George, 1987). This perspective is reflected in the works of Korte (1978) and Carrasquillo-Morales (1983).

In the context of ethnicity, the implicit premise of all the argu-ments in the literature is that self-esteem is rooted in a matrix of cultural values, with traditional cultures revering and investing special significance on the status of old age. While more modern cultures tend to devaluate the aged (Clark & Anderson, 1967; Clark & Mendelson, 1969).

Newton & Ruiz (1980) stress the importance of the family as a source of support and as a means to maintain the self-esteem of Hispanic elderly. Carrasquillo-Morales (1983) studied the perceived social reciprocity and self-esteem among 182 elderly Barrio Antillean Hispanics and their familial informal networks. His study conducted in New York City failed to support his major hypothesis that exchange relationships with informal support systems, especially the family, would be especially relevant to determining the self-esteem of the elderly. He found levels of reciprocity and self-esteem high. He found self-esteem was related to level of norms of support expect-ations from the informal support networks. Females were found to have the highest levels of self-esteem when they felt that there was a minimum of responsibility on the part of their support group to provide for them.

Linn, Hunter, & Perry (1979) compared the psychosocial adjustment of equal numbers of White, Black, and Cuban (N=283) elderly 65 years of age and older living in Miami. Findings revealed no sex differences in overall adjustment. Strong cultural differences were observed. Elderly Blacks showed the best adjustment when social class and level of disability were held constant. Disability had more of an effect on level of adjustment than social class. Cubans showed the most negative adjustment, most likely because of their cultural displacement from Cuba to the U.S. Most Whites in the sample were transplants to Miami, whereas Blacks in the sample were natives which may account for the differences in the better overall adjustment findings.

In a related study, Korte (1978) compared the social interaction and morale of two groups (N=52) of Hispanic elderly couples in northern New Mexico. One group lived in a rural setting, the other in an urban setting. He found the rural elderly had higher morale scores and higher levels of social interaction with immediate and extended kin, as well as with *compadres*. *Compadres* or godparents are a formalized part of the extended family relationship. The urban elderly with high morale scores participated more with neighbors as a substitute for lessened interaction with immediate and extended kin. Elderly females in both groups were found to have more variable morale scores reflective of greater strain in their social situations.

Blau, Oser, & Stephens (1979) in a comparative ethnic study of 2,122 Anglos, 249 Blacks, and 245 Mexican-Americans age 55 and over found ethnicity to have more powerful effects than age and (in many cases also) SES on educational attainment, timing of role exits, health and disability, social supports, and self-concept. Mexican-American women relative both to Mexican-American men, and to Anglo and Black women were found to be the most isolated from peer relationships, had markedly fewer sources of social support, and were more vulnerable to depression and alienation.

Clark & Anderson's (1980) study focused on the cultural influences in the development of mental disorder. Although their sample (N=435) was not Hispanic, it is reported here for three reasons, the use of a comparative community vs. a hospitalized sample, the focus on ethnicity, and use of self-esteem measures as dependent variables. The subjects were 206 males and 229 females, ages 62-94; nearly half (48%) were under 70. Another one-third were between 70-79. Among hospital subjects, the fact of foreign birth was found to have a negative influence on self-esteem. Among community subjects (N=264), appreciable differences were found in self-perception with Southern Europeans more frequently reporting negative self-attitudes than the remainder of the foreign born, as well as native-born Americans. Females in the community sample reported positive self-views more frequently than males. No sex differences were found in the hospitalized group.

The above study highlights the importance of ethnic identity in mental health and the cumulative stress associated with the acculturation process. Acculturation has traditionally been considered a process that involves the absorption of new values or cultural norms/customs.

Acculturation has been found to be associated with a person's mental health status (Griffith, 1983; Szapucznik & Kurtines, 1980) and levels of social support available (Griffith & Villavicencio, 1985). Padilla and his colleagues (Mena, Padilla, & Maldonado, 1987) found that individuals who immigrated to the U.S. after adolescence (ages 12-14) experience greater levels of acculturative stress and lower self-esteem than those who migrated at a younger age.

As indicated previously, a number of studies suggest that Hispanic elderly women relative to their male peers are found to be isolated from peer relationships, have fewer sources of social support, and are more vulnerable to depression and alienation (Blau, Oser, & Stephens, 1979). This is contradictory to Sotomayor's (1973) and Leonard's (1967) studies which found the woman's role in decision making and advising increasing in old age. Carrasquillo-Morales (1982) also found higher levels of self-esteem in females over 60 relative to male peers when they felt that there was a minimum of responsibility on the part of their support group to provide for them.

In summary, there is a paucity of published research focusing on variables which affect mental health among Hispanic elderly. Self-esteem is an important dimension of a person's mental health. For Hispanic elderly, self-esteem is rooted in the family which traditionally has valued its senior members. The studies reviewed show mixed findings for this family-self-esteem relationship. The authors found many differences in the studies that were identified in this review. The characteristics of population's studied, size of the various samples, and varied research designs pose serious problems for drawing any conclusions on how self-esteem affects adaptation to aging in Hispanics. The works reviewed on acculturation, however, do support findings by Becerra & Shaw (1984) that suggest that ethnicity, cultural differences, and socioeconomic status have an impact on the mental health of Hispanic elderly.

Procedures

Data for the study was gathered via in-person interviews conducted at four locations: Hartford, CT., San Antonio, TX., Northern NM., and McAllen, TX. Interviewers included social work students, as well as teachers, volunteers, and natural helpers.

At each location, two distinct samples were generated. A community sample was selected by probability sampling means. All persons in the community sample were at least age 65 and had lived in the United States for a minimum of 10 years (in Hartford, a five-year minimum was used). An agency sample was selected from client lists of agencies providing services to elderly Hispanics.

Institutional psychiatric facilities were excluded from the agency sample. All clients in the agency sample had been known to the participating agency for a minimum of five years.

A total of 391 interviews were conducted. In 44 interviews, two persons, almost always wife and husband, were interviewed together. This resulted in a total sample of 435 respondents. Fifty percent of respondents were from the community sample (218) and 50% (217) were from the agency sample. All analyses in the current paper are based on the combined sample of 435. Detailed information on sampling procedures is available in the Introduction.

Self-esteem scores are derived from the 10-item Rosenberg Self-esteem Scale. A four-point response scale is used (1 = strongly agree, 2 = agree, 3 = disagree, 4 = strongly disagree) with five items reversed scored. High scores indicate high self-esteem with a score of 40 being the highest possible score. The level of help received from others is measured by counting the number of "yes" responses to "yes-no" questions inquiring whether the respondent receives help in five areas: transportation, housekeeping, shopping, help when ill, and help with important decisions.

The level of biculturalism was assessed via eight questions regarding language usage and preference. Responses were on a five-point scale (1 = English only, 2 = mostly English, some Spanish, 3 = Spanish and English about equally, 4 = mostly Spanish, 5 = Spanish only). The items concerned language used most often, preferred language and preference in music, television, radio, movies, magazines, and newspapers.

Self-rated health was assessed via a five-point response scale (5 = excellent, 4 = good, 3 = fair, 2 = poor, 1 = very poor).

Findings

Self-rated health emerged as the best predictor of self-esteem. Those who rated their self-health highly tended to have high levels of self-esteem, $r = .38$ (N = 371), $p < .01$. Age showed a modest negative association with self-esteem, $r = .09$ (N = 369), $p < .05$. Bi-culturalism was also a very modest predictor of self-esteem. Those indicating language preferences for Spanish tended to respond more positively to self-esteem questions. This relationship bordered on significance, $r = .10$ (N = 223), $p < .07$. The level of help received from others was positively associated with self-esteem, $r = .16$ (N = 296), $p < .01$.

The relationships of dichotomous factors with self-esteem were assessed via t-tests. There was little difference in mean self-esteem between those in the clinical and community samples. In the clinical group, the mean score was 31.7 (N = 178, SD = 4.6). The mean score in the community group was 31.4 (N = 195, SD = 6.0), $t(371) = 0.62$, $p > .05$. Similarly, the levels of self-esteem were similar for men (X = 31.2, N = 129, SD = 5.7) and women (X = 31.7, N = 244, SD = 5.3), $t(371) = -0.78$, $p > .05$., and for those who were married (legally or via consensual union) and not married (separated, widowed, divorced, or single). The mean score in the married group was 32.1 (N = 131, SD = 5.5) as contrasted with a mean score of 31.2 (N = 235, SD = 5.3) in the not married group, $t(364) = 1.42$, $p > .06$. Those who had been robbed in the past two years, evidenced lower self-esteem levels (X = 30.0, N = 80, SD = 5.3) than those who had not (X = 31.9, N = 271, SD = 5.2), $t(349) = -2.82$, $p < .01$.

Ethnic identification was assessed via analysis of variance procedures with multiple comparisons. Those who characterized

themselves as Spanish evidenced the highest self-esteem, while
those who self-identified as Mexican-American tended to score
considerably lower. These findings are presented in Table 1.

Table 1
Self-Esteem as Related to Ethnic Identification

Group ab	X	N	SD
Mexicano	31.9	72	5.26
Mexican-American	28.4	54	5.98
Spanish-American	33.4	106	5.34
Puerto Rican	31.4	90	4.12

a. $F_{(318,3)} = 11.7, p < .01$.
b. Multiple comparison tests using the Student-Newman-Keuls
method revealed statistically significant differences at the .05
level between the following pairs of groups: Spanish-
American and both Mexican-American and Puerto Rican;
Puerto Rican and Mexican-American; Mexicano and Mexican-
American

Discussion

This study of two Hispanic elderly samples, a community and
an agency sample (N=435), conducted in four distinct regions of the
country, offers unique opportunities for making comparisons. This
paper has investigated self-esteem differences in relationship to
acculturation levels, ethnic identification, gender, and type of support system used.

In the discussion that follows, the authors attempt to interpret
the findings in light of the limitations found in the literature. The
reader must be cautioned that in the absence of studies that focused
on the combined specific variables of this study, other works were

included that support the general thrust of this effort, but are different, and therefore limit generalizability.

The findings did not support the authors' hypothesis that subjects who use informal support systems, such as the family, neighbors, or friends would perceive themselves more favorably than subjects using a more formal support system, such as a social agency. The data suggest that subjects in the "community" sample were similar to the "agency" sample. Agency identification had no effect on self-esteem. It has been suggested by Maldonado (1975) and others that the Hispanic family is moving toward developing and strengthening the nuclear family. A number of scholars have found evidence that despite higher rates of joint residence with children, Hispanic elderly place a higher value on independence from their adult children (Markides & Mindel, 1987). With the increasing development of formally provided community support systems, i.e. agencies such as those represented in this study, Hispanic elderly have a vehicle to support their independence which enhances their self-esteem and frees adult children to assume other supportive roles in consort with use of community resources.

The findings suggest that the "agency" subjects were different from the "community" subjects only because the former were using an additional resource system. Wright (1983), in an analysis of a national sample of 1,805 Hispanic elderly, found that the informal support system served as a linking mechanism to the formal support system rather than alternative to the formal system.

A second hypothesis, that females would perceive themselves more positively than would males, was not supported. The authors theorized that males would experience lowered self-esteem resulting from loss of status as a consequence of no longer serving in the bread-winner role and the impact that this would have on the man's sense of masculinity. The self-esteem scores were found to be high for both sexes. This suggests other sources of support were present. One suggestion is the tradition of donism, the practice of designating the title of *don* or *doña* as a sign of respect to the elderly.

The authors' findings do not concur with findings by Carras-quillo-Morales (1982) who found females had higher self-esteem scores when they felt that there was a minimum of responsibilities on the part of their support group to provide for them. Díaz-Guerrero (1967) indicates that an increase in social prestige or status can be accorded Hispanic women simply for their age, or because they are mothers, or simply because they are women.

Another contradictory finding is reported by Blau et al. (1979) in a Texas ethnic comparative study. They found Mexican-American women, relative both to Mexican-American men and to Anglo and Black women, are more isolated from peer relationships, have fewer sources of social support, and are more vulnerable to depression and alienation. The authors infer a relationship of the latter variables to self-esteem. These findings lend support to Díaz-Guerrero's (1967) socio-cultural premises on the Mexican family. He asserts two fundamental propositions: (1) the unquestioned and absolute supremacy of the father; and (2) the necessary and absolute self-sacrifice of the mother. His ideas have influenced much of the literature on the Mexican family.

It is interesting to note that research on gender generally indi-cates women in American society have lower self-esteem which reflects societal values that devalue feminine traits. Huyck (1979) indicates that during the second half of life males in American society decrease in masculinity and females decrease in femininity. Institutionalized sexism, including cultural prescriptions for femininity and masculinity, has a significant detrimental effect upon women's self-esteem throughout life. The results reported here for Hispanics suggest other variables may be influencing the self-esteem in Hispanic women.

These findings would suggest a need to re-examine what is referred to in the literature as the "myth of macho dominance" that is prevalent in portrayals of the Hispanic family. An alternative explanation is found in the works of Díaz-Guerrero (1967) who proposes that the Mexican culture is an affiliative and hierarchical system that prescribes primary power to the father, but also affirms the role of the mother in terms of due love and respect. In the Mexican society, he says, the very young and the elderly hold the highest status. They are given respect, power, and love. The reader may question whether similar values are held by other Hispanic groups. A collaborative study of the above author and Maldonado-Sierra et al. (1958) comparing Mexican and Puerto Rican family values found psychological similarities.

The third hypothesis predicted a positive correlation between subjects' self-esteem and acculturation-level scores. As indicated above, biculturalism proved to be a modest predictor of self-esteem. Those indicating preferences for Spanish tended to respond more positively to self-esteem questions. These findings, contradictory to the study hypothesis, support Buriel's (1984) findings on immigrants from Mexico. He indicates that those individuals who maintain their traditional Mexican culture and identity have a more positive self-image and feel more positive about their ethnic group than their counterparts who attempt to shed their traditional Mexican culture.

The literature supports the findings that Hispanics generally prefer speaking Spanish. Of course, there are advantages and disadvantages to retaining one's native language without acquiring fluency in the English language. A number of scholars note that the continued use of Spanish by Hispanics retards acculturation, leads to isolation, and handicaps the elderly in use of social services. Sotomayor (1973) points to the positive effects of unilingual Spanish for the elderly. She believes the use of Spanish serves to strengthen bonds among members of the Hispanic community and has the effect of insulating older Hispanics from negative conflictual messages that are associated with group behavior when a dominant and a minority culture interact.

A fourth hypothesis, that subjects of Mexican ancestry would perceive themselves more positively than their Puerto Rican counterparts, was not supported. The findings indicate that those who characterized themselves as Spanish evidenced the highest self-esteem while those who self-identified as Mexican-American tended to score considerably lower.

García (1982) proposes that ethnicity affects the maintenance of cultural traditions, helps organize a social structure, offers opportunities for mobility and success, and allows individuals the opportunity to enhance their self-concepts in a large, impersonal society. The subjects in this study resided in four distinct regions of the United States. All of the subjects were identified in areas with a high concentration of Hispanics. The authors suggest that some differences found can be explained as a function of ecological factors such as proximity to Mexico for Hispanics of Mexican heritage; temporal factors, such as length of residence in this country for Puerto Rican subjects; and the phenomena of anomie for subjects residing in a large urban Texas city. It is interesting to note that subjects with highest self-esteem scores reside in rural communities in New Mexico and South Texas.

Hispanics of Mexican heritage generally have an agrarian background that one associates with a rural lifestyle. This would suggest that for Hispanics, urban living would require considerable adjustments that are stress producing. In a rural community, everyone knows everyone. One holds status just by being a member of the community. In some communities, the community operates as an extended family. Korte (1975) indicates that rural and urban residence, foreign and native birth, education and occupation can create discontinuities in expectations for interpersonal interactions. His study comparing rural versus urban elderly revealed urban elderly showed stronger feelings of social isolation and lower morale. Spanish-speaking subjects from New Mexico are influenced by local history; many are descendants of parents and grandparents who have lived in the area before New Mexico became part of the United States.

Mena et al. (1987) view self-esteem as a personality dimension associated with a person's capacity to respond to a stressful environment. Chan (1977) argues that "an individual becomes vulnerable to negative maladaptive stress reactions by virtue of seeing him/herself in a powerless position. The authors suggest that subjects in this study residing in urban settings experienced more stress than their rural counterparts. This implies that subjects in rural areas

experienced a more supportive environment that affirmed their individual and ethnic identity. Subjects who characterized themselves as
Spanish were more likely to be New Mexico descendants of Spain
who view themselves as superior to their Mexican counterparts.
Historically, New Mexicans have set themselves apart from persons
of Mexican heritage. It was not uncommon for New Mexicans to refer
to Mexicans as *cholos* . This is a term of contempt used to refer to
half-breeds, persons of European and Indian parentage.

Contradictory to the authors' expectations, subjects who identified themselves as Puerto Rican evidenced higher scores of self-
esteem than those who self-identified as Mexican-American. The
authors propose that this is partly explained by the shorter length of
residence for Puerto Ricans in this country. The Puerto Ricans in this
study were relatively newcomers, less than five years, compared to
other subjects who had ten or more years residence. This would
suggest that as a group, they might be experiencing a "high" or
honeymoon reaction to their new environment. The move to mainland USA for these Puerto Rican subjects likely represents an
increase in family and social status from that held in their homeland.
The data indicate that these subjects were less acculturated as might
be expected given their short history in their new community. As
Sotomayor (1973) suggests, the low acculturation level, not knowing
English could have acted as a shield and reinforced the cohesive-
ness of the Puerto Rican community which elevated the self-esteem
of subjects in this group.

It is suggested that the self-identified hyphenated Mexican-
American group with low self-esteem scores were marginal
individuals who view themselves as misfits in both the majority and

Hispanic communities. As minority individuals increase their fluency in English, their interactions with the majority culture are likely to result in value conflicts that are experienced as ethnic identity conflict. To be or not to be part of the majority culture is a dilemma. This naturally impacts a person's self-esteem. As Díaz-Guerrero (1967) explains, "In order to value oneself, a person must feel at ease." People must feel that they took advantage of life opportunities. The opportunity to be bilingual and bicultural is a choice which can be conflictive for minority individuals.

In the process of examining the variable relationships relevant to the four hypotheses that are the focus of this study, the authors discovered two other variables, self-rated health and receiving help from others, that may be of interest to the reader.

As noted earlier, self-rated health emerged as the best pre-dictor of self-esteem. The literature indicates that a large percentage of Hispanics are forced to retire because of health problems. Health for Hispanics, as for non-Hispanic elderly, becomes a central con-cern with declining age. Health affects life-satisfaction, participation in most social roles, how others respond to us, and how we come to view ourselves. As anticipated, the level of help received was positively associated with self-esteem.

In summary, the purpose of this study was to investigate the relationship of self-esteem with level of acculturation, ethnic identi-fication, gender, and type of support system. The analysis revealed biculturalism to be a modest predictor of self-esteem. Those indicat-ing preferences for native language usage, i.e., Spanish, tended to respond more positively to self-esteem questions. A comparison of four ethnic self-identified groupings revealed that those who characterized themselves as Spanish evidenced the highest self-esteem while those who self-identified as Mexican-American tended to score considerably lower. Levels of self-esteem were similar for men and women. There was little difference in mean self-esteem between those subjects in the agency and community samples.

Psychological Strengths of the Hispanic Elderly: A Comparison of Four Communities

Genaro González

While physical health is crucial to social functioning and personal satisfaction, particularly for high-risk groups such as the Hispanic elderly, mental health is equally important (Padilla & Aranda, 1974; Smith, Burlew, Mosley, and Whitney, 1978). Indeed, these two aspects of health can best be regarded as interdependent elements rather than distinct dichotomies. Hispanics in fact have traditionally treated the two elements as components of one entity (Padilla and Ruiz, 1974). In this respect the Hispanic perspective of mental health has been closer to the present-day tenets of mainstream psychology, which for many decades insisted on distinguishing between psyche and soma. Research on the psychological stresses of Hispanics, especially Mexican-Americans, was for the most part not a major concern prior to the 1960s, and the few studies conducted tended to underplay both the existence of psychological stress in this population and the need for professional intervention. For instance, Jaco (1957) examined the utilization rates of certain mental health services and found that Mexican-Americans were less likely to use them in proportion to the rest of the population. From this he concluded that Mexican-Americans in Texas were more likely to

turn to the family in times of personal crisis. The extended family network was thus portrayed as a buffer that insulated the individual from
external stress. When psychological pressures did affect the individual, the family unit served as a therapeutic network of sorts, with
compadres and siblings taking the role of indigenous counselors.

While Jaco's view offered a rather positive depiction of the
Mexican-American family, it also promoted an ultimately negative
assumption: Mexican-Americans underutilized public mental health
facilities because their families provided the necessary intervention. It
took other researchers such as Karno and associates (Karno, 1966;
Karno & Edgerton, 1969) to question Jaco's methodology and conclusions. They posited that the apparent lack of stress-related pathology among Mexican-Americans was the result of culturally-alien
services rather than a lower incidence of mental illness and/or a
preference for folk therapists (e.g., *curanderas* or *comadres*) per se.
Indeed, they expected that, if anything, Mexican-Americans as a
group would experience more than their share of stress-related
pathology. That theme is echoed by Padilla and Ruiz (1974), who
specify a combination of high-stress variables unique to Hispanics.
These include poverty, discrimination, and cultural/linguistic barriers.
These factors, they argue, would lead one to predict even higher
rates of stress-related pathology among Hispanics. When one adds to
this formula the stresses created by age and ageism, the problems
faced by the Hispanic elderly become monumental. Moreover, many
of the Hispanic aged are more likely to confront a higher absolute
degree of the high-stress variables mentioned above; that is, they are
often at a greater economic and linguistic disadvantage than younger

Hispanics. Their vulnerability to stress should therefore be greater (Dowd & Bengston, 1978).

Coping with stress

In the mental health literature two personality variables have served as valuable predictors of adaptive coping among the elderly: perceived mastery and self-esteem (Varghese and Medinger, 1979). Mastery generally examines the degree to which one feels in personal control of one's circumstances and environment, the extent to which one's actions (or inactions) determine rewards and punishments. The concept is related to fatalism and locus of control, but the above authors do note that we cannot assume that "fatalistic" responses among the minority aged are necessarily maladaptive. Citing Korman's (1971) research, they argue that if the minority elderly were more internal (i.e., believe they have greater mastery or personal control over their environment), they might experience even less life satisfaction. In this respect they agree with Weiss (1971) that subjects who have little power over events in their lives and who make little attempt to cope actively may do so to reduce stress.

Although mastery and related variables (e.g. locus of control) tend to be viewed as linearly related to one's development (i.e., mastery increases with age), the relationship may in fact be curvilinear. That is, perceived personal control in the elderly may diminish for assorted reasons.

Similarly, self-esteem, another important component of coping, may also have a curvilinear effect with respect to age. Given the emphasis that our society places on personal autonomy and individual mastery, the Hispanic elderly, with their aforementioned cultural and linguistic barriers, may experience a considerable decline in self-esteem. One would in fact expect more difficulty with mastery, self-esteem, and other measures of psychological adjust-ment among highly urbanized populations, where greater personal independence and self-sufficiency and less access to a family network may be the norm (Miranda, 1984). Varghese and Medinger (1979) also mention several threats to self-esteem which they feel especially impact the minority elderly. Central to a sense of personal worth, they note, is the need for unconditional positive regard from others. Miranda and Ruiz (1981) concede that the amount of research on self-esteem among the Chicano elderly is seriously limited; the empirical panorama for other aged Hispanics appears no different. They do agree, though, that self-esteem for the former group depends in large part on familial status and respect. Their conclusions are based in part on Cuellar's (1978) research, which documents the significance that the Chicano community assigns to elderly status, including the equation of age with wisdom. This study examines mastery and self-esteem among the Hispanic elderly. Following Newton's (1980) caveat that the Spanish-surnamed elderly should not be categorized as a homogeneous population, the data on mastery and self-esteem were analyzed by site (San Antonio, Hartford, New Mexico, and South Texas). Comparisons between males and females were also examined, since research indicated that variables related to stress, mastery, and self-esteem might be affected by gender (Pearlin & Schooler, 1978; Mendoza, 1981).

Method

Subjects were 347 Hispanic elderly men and women selected from four sites: Hartford, Connecticut; San Antonio, Texas; South Texas; and Northern New Mexico. Respondents from the first site were Puerto Rican elderly; those from the remaining three sites were Mexican-Americans.

Participants were asked to answer a questionnaire in either English or Spanish. The Spanish-language version was developed by means of a translation/back-translation method (Brislin, 1970). A scale developed by Pearlin and associates (1981) was used to measure mastery. The instrument consisted of seven items. For each statement the respondent was required to state his or her level of agreement on a four-point Likert scale ranging from strongly disagree to strongly agree. The scale has previously been used with Hispanic subjects to examine personality resources related to coping (Mendoza, 1981).

Self-esteem ratings were obtained using Rosenberg's Self-Esteem Rating Scale (Rosenberg, 1962). Consisting of ten items, the personality scale was used by Mendoza (1981) to complement Perlin's previously mentioned mastery scale. The items in Rosenberg's instrument tend to cluster into two factors: self-esteem and self-denigration, or the extent to which one holds positive or negative self-attitudes, respectively.

Results
A. Self-esteem

An analysis of variance was performed on the self-esteem data for preliminary purposes. Scores for males and females were

collapsed for each site, with the four sites serving as levels of the
independent variable. Of the total items on the self-esteem scale, half
were found to cluster around a positive self-esteem dimension.
Responses for the five others were grouped around a self-denigration factor. For purposes of this study, only scores from the first were
included in the ANOVA.

Results were significant at the .001 level (F=13.48, with 3
d.f.). Means for the San Antonio, Hartford, New Mexico, and South
Texas sample were 9.33, 7.10, 7.57, and 6.92, respectively. The
higher a combined score, the greater the tendency to disagree with
self-esteem statements. Thus, the San Antonio sample showed the
least self-esteem, the South Texas sample the most. Scores for the
Hartford elderly were similar to the South Texas sample, followed by
the New Mexico sample, whose mean was almost equidistant from
the two Texas extremes.

A more specific breakdown of the itemized responses on the
self-esteem scale was also conducted. A chi-square analysis was
computed for each item, including those that loaded on the self-
denigration factor. As with chi-squares on the mastery scale items
analyzed below, response frequencies for males and females were
analyzed separately, with the four possible levels of (dis)agreement
collapsed into two post-hoc categories (agree/disagree) to allow for a
more simplified pattern.The first item examined the extent to which
the respondent regarded himself as a person of worth. The chi-
square for males (30.87, with 9 d.f.) was significant at the .001 level.
All of the Hartford males agreed with the statement, as did 97% of the
South Texas sample, contrasted with only 62% of their San Antonio
counterparts. New Mexicans fell in-between (83%). Women were not

as differentiated, but the results were also significant at the .01 level. Again, the Hartford Puerto Rican female respondents were more likely to see themselves as persons of worth, the San Antonio elderly Hispanic women the least.

For the second item, male subjects indicated how much they agreed with the statement, "I have many good qualities". Once more, San Antonio males showed the least agreement (76%), all but one of the New Mexico males agreed (96%), and all of the South Texas and Hartford males agreed with the item (p=.01). Results for elderly Hispanic females followed virtually the same pattern.The first self-denigration item on the scale was significant at the .001 level (chi-square value of 32.12, with 9 d.f.). While only 17% of the South Texas and 19% of the New Mexican men were inclined to label themselves as failures, slightly over one half of the San Antonio males did so. Less than a third of the Puerto Rican males assessed themselves as such. The respective frequencies for women were also in the same order and approximated the male samples, with one important exception: less than a third of the San Antonio women considered themselves failures.

An item comparing self-competence vis-a-vis others was significant for elderly men, with a chi-square value of 24.18. Again, San Antonio males were least likely to perceive themselves as competent, while Puerto Rican and South Texas males had a more positive self-perception (86% and 80%, respectively). Differences for elderly Hispanic women were less striking, although again the Hartford and South Texas samples perceived themselves as more competent (85% and 82%, respectively). San Antonio women, though, were in fact slightly more positive than New Mexican women

(76% vs. 73%, respectively).

Another self-denigration item reflecting a lack of pride was also significant for both men and women at the .0001 level. Both San Antonio samples had the highest agreement in their respective gender groups (70% for men, 52% for women). Males from the Hartford and South Texas samples (21% and 27%, respectively) agreed the least; that is, they indicated greater self-pride, with New Mexican males again falling in-between (43% agreeing). An item that stated "I feel good about myself" received agreement from 95% of the Puerto Rican men, 95% of the New Mexican men and 90% of South Texas males. Again, San Antonio males were the least likely (41%) to agree with this positive self-esteem item; the chi-square value was 35.76; p=.0001. Among elderly Hispanic women, the San Antonio sample also had the least agreement, but their self-assessment was considerably higher than that of their male counterparts on this item.

Asked to what extent they felt satisfied with themselves, both San Antonio men and women were the least likely to feel this way; 67% of the men and 86% of the women agreed. Chi-squares for both groups were significant at the .005 level.

In several ways agreement on the remaining three items of the self-esteem scale did not conform to the above patterns for the four groups. Elderly Puerto Ricans were the most likely to express a need for greater self-respect (86% and 80%, respectively). New Mexicans felt the least need (13% for males, 22% for females). Chi-squares for both males and females were significant at the .0001 level, as were analyses for the items that follow.

Puerto Rican men and women were also quite inclined to feel useless at times. Although their frequencies of agreement fell short of those of the San Antonio groups, they nonetheless went counter to their overall pattern of positive self-esteem on earlier comparisons. In each case the South Texas samples were the least inclined to feel useless.

Similarly, agreement rates for the two San Antonio samples and both Hartford samples were rather close and at the higher end of the continuum. Elderly women in each group, though, were less inclined toward self-denigration than were the men. Moreover, both males and females in New Mexico had the lowest self-denigration frequencies on this particular item (21%), followed closely by South Texas men and women.

B. Mastery

Respondents were asked to indicated their degree of agreement with seven items on a perceived mastery scale. Level of agreement with each statement ranged from "strongly agree" to "strongly disagree". A composite score for each respondent was then combined from the seven items, and an ANOVA was computed, combining scores for males and females in each site. The four sites then served as levels of the dependent variable. ANOVA results were significant at the .01 level, with South Texas respondents (males and females) showing the highest perceived mastery (18.71), the San Antonio sample the lowest (14.16). Means for the Hartford and New Mexican samples were almost identical--17.40 and 17.38, respectively.

In addition to the ANOVA, chi-squares were calculated for each mastery item by site, with males and females analyzed separately. The first item examined whether the respondent felt that there was no way of solving some of his or her problems. New Mexican males were most likely to agree with this view (83%), followed by San Antonio men (79%). South Texas males expressed the least pessimism (53%), followed by Hartford men (59%). South Texas women were also the least pessimistic, with San Antonio women expressing the greatest lack of mastery.

Similarly, both San Antonio samples felt the most pushed around by others, albeit women to a lesser degree (63% vs. 76%). New Mexicans were the least likely to agree--with women again less so than men (17% vs. 20%)--followed by the South Texas subjects. The results were significant at the .002 level for men and at the .0001 level for women. The San Antonio elderly were also more likely to feel they had little control over the events in their lives, while Puerto Ricans perceived greater control over their circumstances. Frequencies for Puerto Rican males were identical (53% agreeing), while 80% of the San Antonio men expressed sentiments of externality.

In declaring that there was little that they could not do, South Texas males (80%) and females (93%) were the most optimistic; their San Antonio counterparts, by contrast, felt the least in control (40% and 57%, respectively). Puerto Ricans followed South Texans, with attitudes more similar to the latter than to the New Mexican sample. Chi-squares were significant at the .003 level for elderly men, the .001 level for women.

Both San Antonio groups were also most likely to feel helpless when dealing with life's problems. In fact, the men were almost three times as likely to feel incapable of coping as the best adjusted group, South Texas men; the chi-square value was 49.43, significant at the .0001 level. Here, however, Puerto Rican men and women rivaled the San Antonio sample when it came to a sense of despondency over personal problems.

The Hispanic elderly of San Antonio were also the least likely to agree that whatever happened in the future was most probably their own doing, although the percentage of San Antonio women (68%) was more than twice that of men. Some 96% of the New Mexican men and 84% of the women felt considerable control over their future, followed by the South Texas and Hartford samples. Chi-squares for both males and females were significant at the .0001 level.

Finally, 80% of San Antonio men and 75% of the women from that site felt that they could do very little to change important aspects of their lives. This group contrasted with South Texas men, of whom only 57% felt the same way. It should be noted that the chi-squares for males only approached significance (p=.09) for this item. For women, though, results were significant at the .004 level.

Discussion

The review of the literature in the chapter's introduction mentioned how certain high-stress indicators such as poverty, discrimination, and differences in culture and language may exacerbate problems of living for Hispanics. These factors would seem especially applicable to elderly Hispanics, whose socio-economic limitations and lack of assimilation should make them more susceptible to stress and assorted psychological complications, including lower self-esteem and lack of mastery. Yet to a large extent such predictions were not borne out, at least not to the degree nor in the direction one might expect. For instance, the South Texas and Puerto

Rican samples had on the whole the best psychological profile with respect to mastery and self-esteem. Yet data from the same samples but analyzed elsewhere show that these two groups have the highest poverty background: the South Texas sample lives in one of the country's most economically depressed sites, where racism has been a historical reality, and the Puerto Rican respondents rivaled those of the South Texas sample in their reporting of annual income. Moreover, a cursory analysis of group scores on the acculturation index (examined and discussed in greater detail elsewhere in this book) found that the above two groups tended to be the least assimilated. Theoretically this would place them at greater psychological risk, but such was not the case.

What these findings suggest is that we need to be more cautious in positing the impact of high-risk stress factors on the Hispanic elderly population. Only by specifying the parameters of poverty, discrimination and the like, only by analyzing how stress factors interact with each other, can we pinpoint interfaces that will be useful in the long run. For the time being these preliminary findings leave one with a sobering thought: reality is complex. It is not enough to posit an array of high-stress variables and expect them to affect a population in an incremental, linear fashion. Unfortunately, the results cannot be compared to responses of Anglo elderly. Nonetheless they reveal interesting intra-group similarities and differences. There was, for instance, considerable heterogeneity among the three Mexican-American samples, giving credence to the warning that one must take regional differences of this group into account, rather than assume that the Mexican-American elderly are identical throughout Southwestern communities. Of special note were the striking differences in mastery and self-esteem scores of the two Texas samples--San Antonio and South Texas--showing the heterogeneity that exists within the same state. In truth a more precise designation for the "South Texas" sample would be "Rio Grande Valley", since San Antonio is commonly considered a South Texas community; yet this geographical proximity only serves to emphasize the diversity.

The hypothesis of intra-ethnic heterogeneity was supported by the data, but from these results one might speculate a bit further. Due to the limited range of variables analyzed for this chapter, pin-pointing the reasons for the South Texas/San Antonio differences is beyond the scope of this paper. Still, even minimal insight into the two communities suggests one plausible inference: the combination of urbanization and proximity to the mother (i.e., Mexican) culture.

Life in a highly urbanized community such as San Antonio may have a pejorative impact on the mental health of the Hispanic elderly, a point that Maldonado (1975) and Miranda & Ruiz (1981) take into account in their overview of research in this area. To the extent that this is true, the obverse may occur in a more rural, agri-culturally-based community like the South Texas one.

The second component of the thesis mentioned above involves geographic proximity to the mother culture, in this case contact with Mexico. The South Texas sample lives in a border community, the San Antonio sample does not, and this may be important in several ways. Being close to Mexico may result in a greater retention of the mother tongue and customs, and this cultural saturation may help attenuate the estrangement of living in a cul-turally different country. As was mentioned elsewhere in the study and elaborated in another chapter, the San Antonio elderly were consistently more acculturated than the South Texas sample. In addition to cultural reinforcement, proximity to the border may contribute to a more positive psychological orientation by way of relative deprivation. As Lazarus (1978) points out in his analysis of coping with stress, cognitive appraisal is essential to understanding how and how well an individual deals with problems of living. Thus, the objective fact of living in an economically depressed environment (e.g., the border area) does not in and of itself create stress. Rather, the individual's assessment of his situation is the key, and it is conceivable that many of the South Texas Hispanic elderly may be comparing the course of their lives not with middle-class Anglo elderly but with Mexican elderly, with whom they may share a greater cultural affinity.

If this is the case, objective economic depression perhaps does not translate into subjective mental depression or other manifestations of stress, such as feelings of powerlessness and inadequate self-esteem. Instead, a certain sense of fortunateness may take their place, the perception that although they live in poverty, they are on the average economically better off than most elderly who live south of a border that separates two countries with marked discrepancies in the distribution of wealth. Thus, even though the Hispanic elderly in South Texas ranked among the poorest in the sample (along with Puerto Ricans), their greater opportunity for contact with the mother culture may provide an enhanced cultural, and hence, self-identity as well as an alternate basis of comparison for their deprivation.

The profile of the Puerto Rican elderly in Hartford also conforms quite well to the thesis proposed above. Along with the

South Texas sample, the Hartford elderly generally scored well on the self-esteem and mastery scales; this despite two other characteristics (analyzed in another chapter) that they shared with South Texas Chicanos: low income level and low acculturation indices. Once more one notes that poverty and cultural/language barriers are not necessarily associated with low indicators of mental health and adjustment. Here again contact with the mother culture may provide insights. While the geographical distance between Puerto Rico and the mainland may be a potential barrier to preserving cultural roots, Puerto Rican communities in the U.S. have nonetheless been able to maintain intimate contact with their homeland through a system of cross-migration facilitated by modern air travel (Gann & Duignan, 1986). Indeed, the residence period for the Hartford sample had to be modified in order to compensate for their briefer duration in the United States.

Thus, the Hartford elderly quite possibly managed to maintain close contact with their mother country, which could lead to reinforcement of group/self identity and the utilization of relative deprivation in assessing their status. If this in fact is the case, a more complex group portrait of the Hispanic elderly emerges. On the one hand, one sees considerable diversity within a subgroup (i.e., Mexican Americans) on the two variables of psychological strength, which cautions us against oversimplifying at the subgroup level, much less at the group level. On the other hand, one cannot ignore similar patterns of attitude and conduct shared by South Texas Mexican Americans and Hartford Puerto Ricans subgroups of the Hispanic elderly. This would suggest that despite apparent differences in the historical realities and cultural experiences of both

Hispanic subgroups, certain dynamics centered around bonds with the mother country may in fact provide a common ground.

The chapter began with a brief review of the literature on stress and Hispanics, particularly the elderly. In truth, one must use the concept with caution (Barrera, Zautra & Baca, 1984). In the last few years stress has become a psychological catchword, sometimes synonymous with anxiety. Indeed, some researchers such as Lowen-thal, Thurner, & Chiriboga (1975) operationally define stress in terms of anxiety level. More often it is viewed as a more precise construct than its antiquated cousin, anxiety.

But, in a very real sense both constructs are first and foremost abstractions, attempts to categorize assorted external and internal forces that result in vague subjective states. As with the concept of anxiety, stress runs the risk of reification; and as with anxiety, stress may ultimately be discarded by those who have sought to explain too much with the concept. The recent preference for the stress construct over anxiety may have to do with the former's greater emphasis--at least in theory--on external forces, whereas anxiety was viewed as a more intrapsychic construct.

In truth, the investigation of external factors that affect the Hispanic elderly's psychological well-being has been more theoretical than actual. As Miranda (1981) indicates, the neglect of explanatory factors external to the individual remains a major impediment to insights into the Hispanic elderly.

In addition, a distinction must be made between distress, which is dysfunctional, and eustress. All too often researchers assume that all stress is detrimental. That negative perception fails to take into account the fact that the absense of optimal, healthy stress which makes life challenging and worthwhile may pose a psychological threat as serious as that of distress.

Another reason why we often view stress in a negative light derives from the tendency to associate the term with cognitive overload. But, an individual may also experience problems in living when his environment is at the opposite end of the input continuum--that is, when sensory deficit exists. This distinction especially applies when addressing stress among the elderly, since the problem for many aged may consist of insufficient sensory enrichment rather than a surfeit. Some researchers may assume that the cognitive and sensory surplus that characterizes the lives of certain middle-aged, middle-class, working professionals (e.g., themselves) describes the same type of stress that the elderly face in everyday living. To reduce those sorts of ageist assumptions and replace them with more realistic descriptions of what constitutes mundane stress for the elderly, we must emphasize research that investigates the everyday world of the elderly from a more subjective and in-depth perspective (Gonzalez, 1982). Therefore, future studies of psychological strength in the Hispanic elderly must examine stress within the context of coping and the individual's perception of his social reality.

Life Satisfaction Among the Hispanic Elderly

*Delores Reed-Sanders, Robert Wrinkle,
and Hermila Anzaldua*

The literature suggests that significant variables associated with life satisfaction may be classified into four models. There are factors which focus on psychological, sociological, cultural, and background variables. Psychological resources are personality characteristics that persons may draw upon to help them confront events and objects within their environment. These resources, residing within the self, may serve as buffers to life strains and enhance the degree of life satisfaction (Perlin, et al., 1981). In their classic study of coping, Perlin & Schooler (1978) identified three psychological variables: self-esteem, self-denigration, and mastery associated with the reduction of role strains.

Other research on life satisfaction has used models primarily focused on variables extrinsic to the individual, such as social support, environmental barriers, and family involvement (Holahan & Holahan, 1987; DeJong, et al., 1984; Osberg, et al., 1983; LaRocco, et al., 1980). Social support is an important factor for Mexican-American elderly. Sotomayor (1973) noted that Mexican-American elderly are active, viable members of the family system. Similarly, Martínez (1981) found that support was not one-sided, but involved both receiving and giving. Markides, et al. (1986) also found that Mexican-American elderly were involved in strong helping networks with their children who themselves depend upon them for support. Social support exerts considerable impact upon life satisfaction.

Cultural factors have been shown to influence life satis-faction. Wrinkle, de la Garza, & Polinard (1987) examined the influences upon political attitudes of minorities and noted that cultural variables rather than socio-economic status are better predictors of political attitudes. Ethnicity has been examined as a viable resource in later life, for the elderly may draw upon their culture to enhance their degree of life satisfaction (Simic, 1985). In contrast, Dowd & Bengston (1978) noted that elderly of minority groups are frequently in a double jeopardy situation resulting from both their aged and minority status.

Background variables may also affect life satisfaction. In their study of life satisfaction among disabled adults, Osberg, et al. (1987) examined age, sex, marital status, income, and functional capacity. They found functional capacity to be the best predictor, explaining approximately 40 percent of the variance. Markides & Martin (1979) found health status and activity to be the best predictors of life satisfaction.

The purpose of this study was to investigate whether four models of variables--psychological, sociological, cultural, and back-ground--have a significant effect upon the life satisfaction of older Hispanics.

Methods:
The Sample

The sampling procedure and data for this analysis is described in the introductory chapter. Of the total sample of 347 respondents, 68.6% (238) were females and 31.4% (109) were males. The ages ranged from 62 to 97 with a median age of 73 years. Respondents who lived alone were 65.7% (228) of the sample while 25.2% (87) lived with others. Only 9.2% (32) lived with a spouse. More than half of both females and males were born outside the United States; however, all of the sample had resided in the United States for at least five years.

Variables

The dependent variable, life satisfaction, was measured by the 13-item scale developed by Neugarten, Havighurst, & Tobin (1961). The scoring was on a 3-point scale of agree, don't know, and disagree. The scale has established validity and reliability for this sample (Markides & Martin, 1979; Adams, 1969).

The psychological variables were self-esteem, self-denigration, and mastery. Self-esteem refers to the degree of positiveness of attitude toward self. The scale was developed by Rosenberg (1965) and factored by Perlin & Schooler (1978). The 5-item scale was scored from strongly agree to strongly disagree and was dichotomized as high self-esteem (0-10) and low self-esteem (11-20). Self-denigration refers to the extent in which one holds negative attitudes toward self and was measured on a 4-item scale with responses of strongly agree to strongly disagree. The resulting scale ranged from 4 to 16 and was dichotomized into high self-denigration (0-8) and low self-denigration (9-16). Mastery is a scale developed by Perlin & Schooler (1978) and refers to the extent to which life-chances are considered to be under one's control as contrasted to being fatalistic. The 7-item scale was scored on a 4-point basis ranging from strongly agree to strongly disagree. The scores ranged from 7 to 28 and were dichotomized as low mastery (0-14) and high mastery (15-28).

Three cultural variables were used: Hispanic group, generation since immigration, and biculturalism. Hispanic group was operationalized in terms of site, e.g., Hartford, Connecticut was a Puerto Rican sample; San Antonio, Texas, an urban Mexican-American sample; McAllen, Texas, a rural Mexican-American sample, and northern New Mexico, rural New Mexicans. The generation since immigration variable was dichotomized with first and second generations scoring 0 and third or more generation scoring 1. The biculturalism variable was adapted from an acculturation scale for Mexican-Americans (Cuellar, Harris & Jasso, 1980) and refers to the relative use of the English and Spanish languages. The 8 items were scored from 1 to 5 and dichotomized as more biculturalism (0-16) and less biculturalism (17-40).

Four sociological variables were used to measure social support: help received, help given, visits, and trust. The help received variable was a 5-item scale of items covering such aspects as having someone to provide transportation, to make minor household repairs, to care when ill, and to help with housekeeping and shopping. Responses were coded 1 (yes) or 2 (no). The scale had an alpha reliability coefficient of .79. The scale was dichotomized as receiving help (5-7) and no help received (8-10). The give help scale consisted of five items which was scored on a 4-point basis from always to never. The help given scale covered items such as baby-sit for grandchildren, provide counseling when children have problems, take grandchildren into house, look after son or daughter when ill, and provide financial help to children. The scale had an alpha reliability coefficient of .75 and was dichotomized as giving help (0-10) and not giving help (11-20). The social support variables of visit and trust were operationalized by asking the respondents if there were people they knew well enough to visit and did they have someone to trust. The responses were no one (0) and yes, some-one (1).

Background variables were: age, gender, health, and religiosity. Respondents were asked to rate their health on a scale of 1 (very poor) to 5 (excellent). The responses were dichotomized as poor health (1-3) and good health (4-5). The religiosity variable was a self-reported rating of how religious the respondents felt them-selves to be, ranging from against religion (1) to quite religious (5). The responses were dichotomized as low religiosity (1-3) and high religiosity (4-5).

Analysis

The analysis proceeded in three steps. First, a correlation was used to estimate multicollinearity among the independent variables. Second, a stepwise multiple regression was used to estimate the relationship between the independent variables and life satisfaction for the entire sample and by site. Third, a stepwise multiple regression was used to estimate the relationship between the independent variables and the dependent variable, mastery.

Table 1.

Inter-Correlations Among Psychological, Cultural, Sociological, and Background Variables

	Age	Gender	Sellf-Esteem	Self-Denigra-tion	Religio-sity	Mastery	Self-Rated Health
Age	–						
Gender	-.02 (343)	-- –					
Self-Esteem	.06 (317)	-.01 (320)	– --				
Self-Deni-gration	-.07 (102)	.09 (104)	-.47** (99)	-- –			
Religio-sity	.10* (342)	.16** (346)	-.09 (319)	.03 (103)	– –		
Mastery	-.10* (309)	.02 (312)	-.50** (297)	.54** (100)	.06 (311)	– --	
Self-Rated Health	-.02 (343)	.01 (347)	-.35** (320)	.28** (104)	.00 (346)	.31** (312)	-- --
Trust	-.13** (337)	-.11** (341)	-.02 (315)	.01 (102)	-.08 (340)	-.04 (308)	-.08 (341)
Genera-tion	.03 (334)	-.06 (338)	.06 (315)	.17* (103)	-.14** (338)	-.03 (308)	-.03 (338)
Life-Satis-faction	-.06 (307)	.00 (311)	.48** (296)	-.52** (94)	-.14** (311)	-.52** (291)	-.33** (311)
Bi- Cultura;ism	.03 (215)	-.06 (218)	-.10 (211)	.12 (72)	.16** (218)	.17** (206)	-.06 (218)
Visit	-.08 (313)	-.08 (317)	-.22** (297)	.18* (93)	.06 (316)	.18** (290)	.15** (317)
Receives Help	-.14** (250)	-.06 (253)	-.06 (241)	.31** (85)	-.07 (252)	.04 (235)	.04 (253)
Gives Help	.11 (191)	.11 (192)	.13* (178)	-.18 (50)	-.01 (191)	-.06 (169)	.00 (192)

Table 1. (continued)
Inter-Correlations Among Psychological, Cultural,Sociological, and Background Variables

	Trust	Genera-tion	Life-Satis.	Bi-Cultu-ralism	Visit	Rec'd Help	Give Help
Age							
Gender							
Self-Esteem							
Self-Deni-gration							
Religiosity							
Mastery							
Self-Rated Health							
Trust	— —						
Genera-tion	-.03 (333)	— —					
Life Satisfaction	-.03 (306)	.05 (308)	— —				
Bi-Cultu-ralism	.08 (215)	-.22** (218)	-.09** (209)	-- —			
Visit	-.05 311)	.19** (311)	-.29** (290)	-.08 (206)	-- —		
Receives Help	.09 (250)	.13** (249)	.09 (230)	.09 (230)	-.02 (229)	-- --	
Gives Help	.11 (188)	-.17** (186)	.08 (171)	.08 (171)	-.13* (182)	-.03 (146)	— --

Findings

Before independent variables may be used in a regression equation, a test for multicollinearity must be done. If the independent variables are highly intercorrelated, a regression analysis cannot be performed (Nie, et al. 1975). Markides & Martin (1979) warn that predictors must be examined carefully to ensure that they, themselves, are not measurements of life satisfaction and be highly intercorrelated. A Pearson correlation analysis of the 15 independent variables was used to test for multicollinearity.

As noted in Table 1, mastery, self-esteem, and self-denigration were found to be highly intercorrelated (-.50 and .54); therefore, self-esteem and self-denigration scales were dropped from the analysis. No independent variables with an intercorrelation of above .35 were used in the analysis. The results of the equation are shown in Table 2.

Table 2.
Stepwise Multiple Regression of Psychological,Sociological, and Background Variables On Life Satisfaction

Variable	Multiple Regression	Beta	R^2
Mastery	.492	-.492	.242
Social Support--Visit	.523	-.178	.273
Self-Rated Health	.544	-.159	.296
Age	.566	-.158	.320
Biculturalism	.581	-.132	.337

A stepwise regression was used to isolate a subset of the independent variables which would provide an optimal prediction equation. Independent variables are entered only if they have significant F ratios. The independent variable that explains the greatest amount of variance in the dependent variable is entered first. The variable that explains the greatest amount of variance in conjunction with the first will enter second. This step-by-step process continues for all significant variables. In other words, the variable that explains the greatest amount of variance unexplained by the variables already in the equation enter the equation at each step (Nie, et al. 1975).

As noted in Table 2, the equation resulted in five significant variables having an R square of .337. Approximately 34% of the variation in life satisfaction was explained by the total equation. The first variable to enter the equation was mastery. It accounted for almost 75% of the total explained variance with an R square of .242 and a Beta of -.492. Because the mastery scale was coded as low equaling low mastery and the life satisfaction scale was coded as low equaling high life satisfaction, the relationship of high mastery contributing to high life satisfaction resulted in a negative Beta. The pattern of relationship was inverse. The next item to enter the equation was the social support--visit variable. This variable had a Beta of -.178 and explained about 3% additional variance. The sign of the Beta indicated that those with more visits enjoy higher life satisfaction. The third variable in the equation was self-rated health which explained an additional 3% variation. The item had a Beta of -.159, indicating that those with perceived good health had higher life satisfaction. The next two variables were age with a Beta of -.158 and biculturalism with a Beta of -.132. Each of these variables explained an additional 2% variation. The five variables in the equation explained 34% of the variance.

Since the overall sample represented sub-groups of urban Puerto Ricans in Hartford and Mexican-Americans in rural areas of New Mexico and South Texas and the urban area of San Antonio, a step-wise regression was run on each of the sites in order to assess the impact of these differing sub-groups. These regressions were done on much smaller samples and somewhat different results would be expected due to the size alone. However, the analyses show no substantial differences from the total sample. The results are in Table 3.

The first variable which entered all four equations was mastery. As for the entire sample, mastery explained more of the variance than any other variable. The most striking differences among the equations for the total sample and the sub-groups are the number of variables to enter the equations. Hartford and South Texas had three variables, San Antonio had two and New Mexico had only one variable. The explained variance for the sites were: 26% for Hartford, 37% for New Mexico, 31% for San Antonio, and 23% for South Texas. For each of the sub-groups and for the combined sample, the psychological variable of mastery was the primary explanatory variable of life satisfaction for this sample of Hispanic elderly. The variations that did exist among the four equations are interesting, but did not appear to be reflective of culture. In New Mexico, only mastery entered the equation. In San Antonio, self-rated health entered as the second and final variable and explained an additional seven percent variation. In Hartford, age and religiosity entered after mastery and explained an additional 11% of variance. The slight increase of the explained variance was an anomaly which apparently resulted from an interactive effect.

Table 3.
Stepwise Multiple Regression of Psychological,Sociological, and Background Variables On Life Satisfaction for Four Research Sites

Site	Variable	Multiple R	Beta	R^2
Hartford	Mastery	.316	-.316	.100
	Age	.464	-.344	.215
	Religiosity	.506	-.206	.260
New Mexico	Mastery	.610	-.610	.372
San Antonio	Mastery	.486	-.486	.236
	Self-Rated Health	.558	-.295	.311
South Texas	Mastery	.408	-.408	.166
	Generations Since Immigration	.476	-.245	.227

Only in South Texas did a cultural variable enter the equation. Generation since immigration entered as the only variable other than mastery and explained approximately 6% more variation. The Beta was .245 indicating that the more generations since immigration, the greater the life satisfaction. South Texas is a border region and the close proximity to Mexico may account for the significance of a cultural variable.

To understand further the role which mastery played in determining life satisfaction, a regression equation was estimated with mastery set as the dependent variable. As before, self-esteem and self-denigration were dropped because of multicollinearity. In estimating this equation, an attempt was made to control for mastery as an intervening variable in the previous equation. In other words, since mastery was so important in determining life satisfaction, it was important to determine what factors influence mastery. The results of the equation are in Table 4.

As noted in Table 4, the estimated equation was not very productive in explaining variation in the dependent variable of mastery. Only three items entered the equation with self-rated health being the most important, accounting for 9% of the variance. Of the total variation explained (12%) self-rated health accounted for the greatest proportion. This appears to indicate that few of the other independent variables assist in explaining mastery. In other words, mastery did not appear to be an intervening variable between the other types of variables (background, cultural, and sociological) and the dependent variable of life satisfaction.

Table 4.
Stepwise Multiple Regression of Psychological, Sociological, and Background Variables on Mastery

Variable	Multiple R	Beta	R^2
Self-Rated Health	.308	-.308	.095
Social Support (Visit)	.338	.142	.114
Age	.353	.100	.124

Discussion

This analysis of life satisfaction among Hispanic elderly clearly indicated that the mastery variable was of primary importance. The significance holds for all of the sub-groups surveyed. Although some variation was present among the groups, they shared the same dominant attributes in explaining life satisfaction. Previous research (Wrinkle, de la Garza, & Polinard, 1987; Garcia & de la Garza, 1977) has indicated heterogeneity among the Hispanic populations; however, that heterogeneity does not appear to explain life satisfaction. Clearly, mastery is the common, significant, and single factor in explaining life satisfaction. This finding supports the literature which suggests that empowerment of the elderly is one of the most significant influences upon life satisfaction. Further research among this population, as well as other populations, is needed.

Authors' Note:
Partial support for the South Texas component of this research came from the U.S. Department of Education, Minority Institutions Science Improvement Program (MISIP) (grant G008641834) and the Pan American University Faculty Research Council (grant 1571). Since the authors shared equally in each phase of the project, the names are in rotated alphabetical order. MISIP Student Research Assistants Eloisa Carrillo, Thomas Longoria, and Cathie Watkins are gratefully acknowledged.

Life Satisfaction of Older Hispanics

Alvin O. Korte and Robert F. Villa

Introduction

The need to identify predictive factors or variables that influence the sense of well being of Hispanic elderly falls within the broad scope and range of the National Hispanic Council on Aging Research Study objectives. This area of research has immediate application for the clinician, policy analyst, and researcher. One goal is to disseminate this information to practitioners in a language immediately applicable for practice. Professional social workers are called upon to act as teachers, liaisons, facilitators, and mediators in the lives of elderly persons. Therefore, it is important to influence the lives of the elderly in a manner that would eliminate stressors as well as strengthen them individually so that they will be able to cope with similar problems in the near future. Such preventative efforts could stem further dysfunction. Additionally it is important to document psychological, cultural, social, and religious resources used in coping and managing stress caused by problems in living. To accomplish this it is imperative that the social worker understand and use the elderly's informal supportive networks to facilitate equilibrium within their social and cultural environment. Life satisfaction is a major indicator not only of personal well-being, but is also reflective of the person's sense of personal efficacy. As a dependent variable, it acts as a barometer reflecting social and psychological conditions. Just what external social and psychological variables influence life satisfaction with regard to Hispanic elderly has not been extensively documented. This presentation is an initial attempt to map out these parameters.

Life Satisfaction: A Brief Review

Life satisfaction has received considerable attention in social gerontological research. Larsen (1978) reports of thirty years of research on the subjective well-being of older Americans. Larsen's review concludes that these studies are unified by their objective of assessing the affective experience of older persons in terms of a positive-negative continuum. His review asserts that although there are different conceptualizations and measures of the positive-negative continuum, they reveal comparable findings. These studies conclude that there is a relationship between measures of this positive-negative dimension and life experience. "Poor health, low income, and lack of social interaction, among other things, are clearly related to lower expressed satisfaction with life, lower morale, and lower contentment. Further, these negative situational conditions, particularly low income, appear to to be related to a greater vulnerability to the impact of other negative life situational exigencies" (p.109).

There have been numerous attempts to define and measure the psychological well-being of older persons with the goal of conceptualizing an operational definition of "successful" aging. Terms such as adjustment, competence, morale, or happiness and their respective measurement criteria have been used. A number of cogent criticisms of these attempts at definition and measurement have been made. These criticisms were made because they are inextricably involved with value judgements (Neugarten, Havighurst, & Tobin, 1961). One goal of the Kansas City Study of Adult Life was to develop a life satisfaction measure that would use the individual's own evaluations as a point of reference. This measure would be independent of the level of social participation and interaction (Neugarten, et al., 1961). The scale that evolved from these studies is the 20-item Life Satisfaction Index A (LSIA) (Neugarten, et al.,1961). This scale has been prominent as a dependent variable in considerable research activities. Its progeny is the 13-item scale used in the National Hispanic Council on Aging Research Study. This 13-item scale came from the work of a restudy of the 20-item LSIA instrument on a rural Kansas sample. The researchers concluded that similar results could be obtained with a 13-item scale as with the 20-item LSIA (Wood, Wylie, and Schaefer, 1969). This latter scale came to be known as the Life Satisfaction Index Z, LSIZ. Both scales have been studied to determine whether their structure reflects the five components identified by the developers of the scale. Havighurst and his colleagues identified five components in his life satisfaction index. As listed by Atchley, they are:

Zest--showing vitality in several areas of life, being enthusiastic.

Resolution and Fortitude--not giving up, taking the good with the bad and making the most of it, accepting responsibility for one's own personal life.

Completion--a feeling of having accomplished what one wanted.

Self-Esteem--thinking of oneself as a person of worth.

Outlook--being optimistic, having hope.   (Atchley, 1985)

Currently the debate as to what constitutes components of
the global concept of life satisfaction continues to be a topic of
research endeavors. A major issue as to what life satisfaction indices
actually measure, as well as the appropriate combination of items
continues to be a topic of debate. Many of these studies focus on the
structure of the LSIA across varying and different subpopulations
(Hoyt & Creech, 1983, Carp & Carp, 1983, Liang, 1984). It is not the
purpose of this presentation to evaluate the merits of the scale per se,
but to point out that the analysis of its structure will probably continue
to be debated, evaluated, and tested with other subpopulations
(Liang, Tran & Markides, 1988).

A Connection to Clinical Practice and Program Evaluation

As a quality of life concept, life satisfaction can be used as an
organizing framework from which knowledge-oriented researchers
and action-oriented practitioners would have a basis for discourse.
As a basic research concept, quality of life assists in focusing on
conditions under which aging is satisfying or debilitating and in
identifying the resources and coping skills influencing the aging
process (George & Bearon, 1980). Beaver & Miller (1985) point out
that life satisfaction has generally been seen within the context of
activity theory. They argue for a position in which loss of functions is
a central concept. They notice that some people are more successful
in dealing with age-related changes than others. It is therefore
important to consider that some older individuals may be able to hold
on to functional capacities for a longer period of time. However, the
well-elderly may have more social, economic, and psychological

supports than others. The well-elderly bring to the latter stages of life good mental and physical health as well as activities aimed at prevention and a lifetime of successful coping and adaptation. They anticipate needs and problems and are well informed of creative and resourceful means to apply in new situations (Beaver & Miller, 1985).

In the applied area, the life satisfaction concept can be used as a program impact variable affected by service programs and policies on older individuals. Wylie (1970) emphasizes the point that the Life Satisfaction Index Z was useful in evaluating a demonstration program for the aged. The scale she argued gets at the deeper dimensions of the elderly's personality by "striking at social psychological areas of human experience." As a program impact variable, "the LSIZ demonstrates its capacity to record positive and negative change, an important criterion for an evaluative tool" (pp.39-40). George & Bearon (1980) note that the practitioner operates on the same dimension as the program evaluator and that the clinician also sets goals for improving the life quality of an older client.

A life satisfaction scale and a well-formulated theory which would undergrid its foundation would be an important adjunct in research and in the applied areas of program evaluation and direct services to the elderly. What remains to be done is to provide this information in a format that is comprehensible and useful to the practitioner. This must be done in a manner that will facilitate use of the instrument in the administration and interpretation of the data produced.

Life Satisfaction and the Hispanic Elderly

Few studies pertaining to life satisfaction of Hispanic elderly exist. Markides, Martin, & Gómez (1983) note in passing that, except for a few unpublished articles, gerontological researchers have largely ignored this area of study.

Nuñez (1975) compared the social interaction patterns of elderly Anglos and Mexican-Americans using a 3-item scale from the Philadelphia Geriatric Center Morale Scale. He posited that social interaction with the family is a good predictor variable of morale. Mexican-American elderly not only interacted more with familial networks, but their expectation for high level of social interaction can also have a causal effect on high or low morale. He noted that "while at an objective level the [Mexican-American elderly] may be no more socially isolated than his Anglo counterparts, he may well be isolated at a subjective level as evidenced by his significantly lower morale in a situation of unmet expectations" (pp.9-10).

A small New Mexico study using a Spanish translation of the LSIZ scale found that rural elderly had a higher mean morale score than elderly in a small adjoining city. Only locale was statistically significant. Gender and the interactional effects of gender and locale were not statistically significant (Korte, 1982).

Using the 13-item LSIZ as well as a self report measure of life satisfaction Markides, Martin, & Gómez (1983) examined differences between older Mexican-Americans and Anglos in a San Antonio *barrio*. According to their findings on the question "Is this the happiest time in your life?" no differences were observed by ethnicity when socioeconomic status is held constant. A second question asked "On the whole how happy would you say you are?". Mexican-

Americans scored higher on this item than older Anglos irrespective of socio-economic class. Markides et al. (1983) make the interesting point that older Mexican-Americans report being unhappier when compared to Anglos. However, high levels of agreement with the latter item may reflect that the present time is much better to earlier and more difficult years. The additional point is raised that Mexican-American elderly may be insulated from the broader society that views aging in an unfavorable light.

In examining life satisfaction among Mexican-Americans and Anglos, Markides used a health measure which assigned scores per severity of illness. Confinement in bed was also similarly scored. An activity index was constructed which identified frequency of attendance as well as levels of participation. Two measures for socio-economic status included education and monthly family income. Marital status and gender were used as binary variables. A multiple regression analysis found that for Mexican-American elderly the important predictors of life satisfaction were health, activity, and marital status in that order. Anglos, on the other hand, had higher life satisfaction based on activity, health, and education. Markides remarks that the observed differences in health between minority and majority elderly may reflect overall differences in socioeconomic status between the two groups. Educational differences, he suggests, are more important to the older Anglos at the upper ranges in education where more Anglos were concentrated than for Mexican-Americans, who were at the lower end of the education continuum. Thus minimum levels of education must be attained before it affects life satisfaction. He argues that educational attainment for Mexican-American elderly or other populations with minimal education could have significant improvement in managing and functioning in a complex environment. Finally, interaction with kin, which should be different in the two study population, did not show differences. The variable seemed more important for the Anglo elder (Markides, 1980). For additional analysis, consult the Markides & Martin article on a path analytic study of differences between males and females on life satisfaction (Markides & Martin, 1979).

One of the first analyses to study the underlying structure of the 20-item LSIA was conducted by Adams (1969), who found through factor analysis that of the five dimensions, evidence existed for the three factors of mood tone, zest versus apathy, and the congruence component. The fourth factor tapped both congruence, and resolution and fortitude. A fifth factor tapping self-concept did not seem to emerge as posited by Havighurst et al. (1963). Adams concluded that the LSIA provides a "fair estimate of life satisfaction for a small town elderly sample as it does for the urban and rural samples on which it was previously tested" (p.473). The analysis by Wood et al. suggested the 13-item scale LSIZ found a "respectable level" of correlation with other life satisfaction measures available. The argument was made that some validation existed for the scale. Wood et al, suggest that the scale may be appropriate when moderate levels of life satisfaction or morale are expected. They were not as confident about scores for elderly women due to the way data was collected (Wood, et al. 1969).

The availability of advanced statistical procedures such as LISREL have led to renewed interest in the structure of the LSIA. Focusing on subjective well-being as a second order construct or factor was hypothesized to account for the correlations among the three first-order dimension of mood tone, zest, and congruence. The model proposed by Liang (1984) posits that mood tone was composed of the following three items: "I am just as happy as when I was younger," "My life could be happier than it is now," and "These are the best years of my life." Zest was theorized as composed of the following items: "I expect some interesting and pleasant things to happen to me in the future," "The things I do are as interesting to me as they ever were," "I feel old and sometimes tired," and "Most of the things I do are boring and monotonous." Congruence was thought to be reflected by "As I look over my life I am fairly well satisfied," "I would not change my past life even if I could," "I have gotten pretty much what I expected out of life," and "I have gotten more breaks in life than most of the people I know." Some of these items are similar to the ones identified by Adams (1969); see also Table 1 in Liang, (1984).

Using a complex replication of sub-samples, Liang notes that positive self-concept and fortitude do not emerge as hypothesized by Neugarten and her associates (Neugarten, 1961). Instead he found that the hypothesized second-order factor of well-being accounts for the correlations among the three first-order dimensions of the LSIA to include mood tone, zest, and congruence. Despite differing statistical proceedures in the Hoyt & Creech (1983) study, Liang finds similar assignment of items to the three identified dimensions. Despite good replication across the four sub-sample groups he studied, Liang is cautious in pointing to differences in the two studies and in proposing that the scale be studied across groups that vary by age, gender, and race (Liang, 1984).

A recent study by Liang, Tran, & Markides was to determine if seven life-satisfaction items would provide consistent findings with three generations of Mexican-Americans. The three generations were an older generation, a middle-aged generation, and a younger generation. Two items were used to measure mood tone, two for zest, and three for congruence. The seven items constitute three first-order dimensions. A second-order factor, subjective well-being is hypothesized to account for the correlations among the first-order dimensions (Liang, Tran, & Markides, 1988). This is essentially the model developed by Liang (1984) but with only seven of the original eleven items. Several goodness of fit statistical procedures were used which predicted more than an adequate fit of the items in the models. The authors conclude:

> Findings from this research certainly complement those reported in previous studies. First, this analysis offers additional support for the hypothesis that LSI contains three first-order dimensions and that the correlations among them are due to an existence of a second-order factor. ...Moreover, the generalizability of this hypothsis has now been extended to a sample of Mexican-Americans. Second, the generational differences found in this study are, in general, similar to findings that many LSI items do not fit into age-gender invariant scales (Liang, et al. 1988).

This brief review of the literature illustrates the history of efforts to hone the measurement of life satisfaction. It has been an arena that has received considerable research attention and that will probably continue as additional issues are raised. The scale used in the present study is the 13-item. Many of the items in the scale are similar to the seven items in the Liang, et al. study. This is only to suggest confidence in the LSIZ and that it can be used with Hispanics at least in a crude analysis of social and psychological variables.

Method of Analysis

Multiple regression is a multivariate technique for assessing the effects of a multiple number of independent variables on a dependent variable. In effect, the technique is used to predict scores or variance on a dependent variable as a function of one or more independent variables. The 13-item life-satisfaction index LSIZ is the dependent variable of interest in this study. How this variable is concomitantly influenced by such predictor variables as activity, gender, self esteem, and other variables is the central tenet of this study. Multiple regression can be used as a general variance accounting procedure of great flexibility, power, and fidelity in both manipulative and observational research (Cohen, 1968). Nominal level independent variables can be used in multiple regression analysis (Kerlinger & Pedhauzer, 1973). Nominal-level variables are often called "dummy" or binary variables. Basically they are variables that have two values represented by ones and zeros such as coding 1 for rural and 0 for urban. In this study, several binary variables were created as independent variables.

Variable Identification

Fifteen independent variables and one dependent variable were selected for analysis. The 13-item LSIZ (Adams;1969, Wood, Wylie, & Schaefer, 1969) scale was elected to measure the dependent variable. It was scored with one point for each correct answer and a zero for an incorrect answer. The independent variables consisted of COMMUNITY & AGING, MARITAL STATUS, AGE, EDUCATION, INCOME, SATISFACTION, GENERATION SINCE IMMIGRATION, BICULTURATION, RELIGION , RELIGIOUS PREFER-ENCE, ESTEEM, HEALTH, EXPRESSIVE FUNCTIONS, MASTERY, and ACTIVITIES OF DAILY LIVING. Two classes of variables were used to determine overall differences in the samples. Site was used to determine if there were significant differences in life satisfaction between urban and rural residency. All Sites was used in the study to test for regional differences in life satisfaction across all four sites. These two variables were used to select the subgroups for separate regression analysis. The second set of independent variables were used as predictors in the multiple regression analysis. These fifteen predictor variables can be construed as having two characteristics. Some variables reflect psychological resources such as self-esteem and mastery. Others reflect socio-demographic characteristics that mirror social resources like education, income, and ability to manage the social environment in old age.

Site was developed as a binary variable in which subjects from New Mexico and the McAllen/Edinburg area were combined into the rural site with San Antonio and Hartford in the urban category. There were 230 subjects in the rural category and 205 in the urban category. These variables were deemed important in differentiating urban and rural levels of life satisfaction. The second site variable, All Sites, was used in an all inclusive multiple regression equation to ascertain which predictor variables make for differences in life satisfaction across all four sites.

Gender, G1, was considered an important variable because

of the disproportionate number of females in relation to males in the general population. There were 153 males or 35 percent of the total sample. Females numbered 282 or almost 65 percent of the total in planning for the sample, a decision was reached to oversample the females as a closer approximation to actual population counts. Table 1 presents the marital status of the sample.

Table 1.
Marital Status of the National Hispanic Council Respondents

	NA	M	D.	W.	Septd.	Sin.	Consen.	Total
M	3	75	11	39	8	15	2	153
%	0.5	17.4	2.5	9.0	1.9	3.5	0.5	35.3
F	3	79	20	144	16	17	1	280
%	7	18.3	4.6	33.3	3.7	3.9	0.2	64.7
	6	154	31	183	24	32	3	433
%	1.2	35.7	7.1	42.3	5.6	7.4	0.7	100

Most of the females were widowed while most of the males were married. One could postulate that marital status, MS, would be an indicator of life satisfaction. Marital status was treated as a binary variable because of the large proportion of married (154 or 36 percent) comparison to the "other category" which includes those who were divorced, separated, single, or widowed. Five cases had missing data. There were 278 persons in the "other" category.

AGE was used as a continuous variable ranging from forty-nine to ninety years of age. The mean age for the sample was 73.7 years of age with a medium of 73 years and a standard deviation of 7.4 years of age.

Given that the selection of the sample was specifically targeted towards low income, educational levels were similarly low.

The average educational level was in the lower category of 0 to 4 years. Sixty-five percent or 272 persons were in this category followed by 24 percent or 106 persons in the 5 to 9 years of education.

Income level for this sample was similarly low with a modal income between $4000 to $6000, followed by the lower category of $2000 to $3000. There were 143 cases or thirty percent in the first category and 108 cases in the second category. Only eight cases had income levels above ten thousand dollars.

Generation since immigration, GSI, has been a variable of interest to students of the Hispanic family. Since well over fifty per-cent of the cases were first generation, it was deemed important to separate into a binary variable category. First generation elderly were predominantly monolingual and from the Hartford area. The other category consisted of "all other" generations. From the initial analysis, the next largest category consisted of many fifth generation elderly mainly from northern New Mexico.

The variable termed Biculturation, BICUL, does not reflect biculturalism in a pure form, but the preference and ability to handle written media in both Spanish and English as well as preference for Spanish music and television programs over English. Most of the Hartford sample scored highest in this variable which is indicative of greater monolingualism. The northern New Mexicans had the lowest scores in this section of the questionnaire reflecting more ability in both languages. It was thought that higher life satisfaction would be a function of ability to handle an environment in which English is the predominant language.

Religion has long been recognized as an important variable

in the lives of older Hispanics. One item in the questionnaire asked elderly if they had *fe* or "faith". In the initial data analysis, this item had the highest level of agreement across all sites. Only twelve persons responded in a negative way. REL is a variable that measures levels of religious orientation with the following categories: "against religion," "a little religious," "religious like others," and "quite religious." Forty-two percent declared that they were "religious like others," followed by thirty-five percent in the "quite religious" category. The other religious variable is a contrived binary variable from the questionnaire that asked persons to identify their religious preference. Given that Hispanics are not monolithically Catholic, this variable, termed RELPREF, placed all Catholics in one category and all other religions into another category. There were 355 Catholics in the sample or eighty-two percent, with eighty persons in the other category.

Self-esteem, or ESTEEM, is measured by the 10-item Rosenberg scale (Robinson & Shaver, 1973). The average response was 7.15 with a medium of 8.0 and a standard deviation of 2.3. Seven percent or thirty persons had low scores of three and below while the "high" group of 276 had scores of seven and above. The overall impression was that persons in the four sites had better than average self-esteem scores.

Self-rated health was a composite score that came from a variety of scales which consider number of days ill in the prior year, days in hospital, a self-rated scale, and a perception of change in health status. The possible high score was twenty-five. The mean score was 16.9 with a medium of 18 and a standard deviation of 4.18.

Expressive Functions, EXP, was one of many variables

tapping the expressive function. EXP is an attempt to determine the number of contacts the elderly person or couple visited with relatives or others during a given period of time. The categories are "no one" checks on them, someone comes daily, weekly or at other time time period. Fifty-five percent or 242 saw someone daily, while twenty-one percent or ninety-three saw no one, and nineteen percent or eighty-six persons were visited by someone at least weekly. A small group of ten were seen at other intervals.

The Mastery scale found in the Pearlin and Schooler (1978) work is a 7-item scale that measures psychological resources in coping with life strains. Specifically the scale is concerned with the "extent to which one regards one's life-chances as being under one's control in contrast to being fatalistically ruled" (p 5). This scale is identified as MASTERY in the analysis and has a high possible score of seven.

Satisfaction is a binary variable derived from the question "Taking everything into consideration, how satisfied are you with life at present?" The vast majority of respondents described being "pleased with life at present." Thus 344, or seventy-nine percent, indicated in the affirmative. A remaining number or sixty-four persons, or fourteen percent, gave a variety of responses ranging from being "lonely," "depressed," "everything cost so much," and "worry about crime." Due to its high correlation with LSIZ, this variable was not used in the regression analysis.

Activities of daily living, or ADL, was modified from the ADL scale in the OARS instrument (1975). This scale takes into account the ability to perform household chores, ability to walk, shop, care for self, and other functional chores around the house. A possible high

score of twenty-five characterizes fully functional individuals. The
mean for the group was 21 with a medium of 23 and a standard
deviation of 4.36. Most of the respondents scored in the high range
of the scale.

The sample was further dichotomized into "agency" and
"community" groups, or CA. The rationale for selecting respondents
from an agency and non-agency population is based on expectations
that each would provide distinctively different data in relation to
questions about stress, familial relationships, support networks, and
coping styles.

Findings

A multiple regression analysis was run with all the sites
included. Of the fifteen predictor variables, G1 enters into the regression model followed by MASTERY, HEALTH, and RELIGION. G1, or
gender, has a high F value of 262.60. The zero order coefficient
equaled -.614. The negative sign of the coefficient indicates that
males were more likely to have lower life satisfaction than females.
Mastery has a positive zero order correlation coefficient of .225 and is
also statistically significant. High levels of Mastery are associated
with high levels of life satisfaction. HEALTH is also positively
associated with life satisfaction for the overall sample across all sites.
RELIGION as a measure of religious orientation also has a
statistically significant zero order correlation with life satisfaction.

It is of interest to speculate on why these variables enter the
model. It can be posited that gender differences are correlated with
life satisfaction. Perhaps harsher life experiences for the male means
lowered morale and life satisfaction in old age. Being old and male

may mean less satisfaction. Perhaps harsher life experiences for the male means lowered morale and life satisfaction in old age. Being old and male may mean less roles and meaningful social activites and hence less life satisfaction. The sense of mastery and feeling that one is able to cope is a psychological resource that would seem to be naturally related to life satisfaction. It is interesting to note that Mastery is the only psychological variable to enter the regression equations. It would seem that health would also be related to gender differences and perhaps this is why it is one of the predictor variables in the model. Finally, Religion is also positively associated with an optimistic and hopeful outlook on life. The converse is also a possibility; less religious orientation and more dissatisfied outlook on life. This might be more indicative of depression in the sense that the outlook would be less satisfaction with life and a sense that not even spirituality matters.

Table 2 below summarizes the major findings in this multiple regression analysis for all the sites combined.

Table 2.
Multiple Regression -All Sites Combined

Variable Entered	F Ratio	D/F	Signif. Level	Mult. R	R^2	Zero Correl.
G1	262.61	1/433	.0000	.6144	.3775	-.614
MASTERY	152.97	2/432	.0000	.6438	.4146	.230
HEALTH	107.75	3/431	.0000	.6546	.4285	.171
RELIGION	84.32	4/430	.0000	.6630	.4396	.244

Multiple R is the correlation of the dependent variable with the independent variables. In the table above the multiple R increases as more variables enter into the model. The large multiple R of .6630 is substantive. The amount of variability explained is given by the multiple R squared. In this case the model explains almost forty-four percent of the variance in the dependent variable.

Site Analysis

There were 205 cases used in this analysis for the urban group and 230 for the rural group. An analysis by urban and rural sites reveals some interesting differences. Several major variables enter into the multiple regression for the urban group. These variables in order of their stepwise entry into the model were G1, HEALTH, MASTERY, REL, and CA. G1 or gender correlated negatively or -.586 with life satisfaction, while HEALTH correlated a positive .276 with life satisfaction. MASTERY, REL, and CA all had positive correlations, .306, .264 and .180 respectively. All zero-order correlations were statistically significant at levels beyond the .01 level. In point of fact most of the zero-order correlations reported in this paper, except as noted, were significant beyond the .01 level.

For the rural group only G1 and MASTERY enter the multiple regression model. Life satisfaction and gender, G1, correlated at -.636, while MASTERY reached significance with a positive correlation of .209. Table 3 summarizes the model's predictor variables.

In analysis of the zero-order correlation coefficients, a coefficient of -.614 of G1 with life satisfaction reveals that males tended to have lower levels of life satisfaction than females. In the initial data analysis, males scored lowest in life satisfaction in San Antonio, followed by Hartford, both urban areas. The highest ranking males in life satisfaction were in the South Texas site. They scored a

Table 3.

Multiple Regression By Urban and Rural Sites

Variable Entered	F Ratio	D/F	Signif. Level	Mult. R	R^2	Zero Correl.
Urban						
G1	106.059	1/203	.0000	.5858	.3432	-.586
HEALTH	68.339	2/202	.0000	.6353	.4035	.276
MASTERY	52.398	3/201	.0000	.6625	.4388	.306
REL	52.398	4/200	.0000	.6773	.4588	.106
CA	35.289	5/199	.0000	.6855	.4699	.180
Rural						
G1	155.056	1/228	.0000	.6362	.4048	-.636
MASTERY	90.064	2/227	.0000	.6652	.4424	.209

full point higher than females in the same site. Males in New Mexico had a mean of 6.30 as compared to 6.06 for females (NHCoA Final Report, 1986). Lower life satisfaction for males is also evident as one of the major predictors even in the site-by-site analysis and in an anlysis by gender that is not reported in this paper.

It is of interest to note the effects that religion and the variable named CA have on life satisfaction. In the case of religion the correlation coefficient is a positive .264. Greater self-perceived religiousity is thus positively correlated with greater life satisfaction. The binary variable termed CA represents two situations. Those who were known to a community agency were coded 1, while those sub-jects coming from sampling in the community were coded 0. Since CA is a positive correlation, those elderly participating in social agency recreational and service programs had higher levels of life satisfaction. This is not to suggest that elderly receiving serivces are better off because there could also be a self selection into agency programs by the elderly themselves. In effect, the well-elderly could also have higher levels of social participation. What is to be surmised is that participation in social and recreational agencies is conducive to higher life satisfaction scores. Table 4 presents a site-by-site analysis of the major variables forming the multiple-regression analysis.

Common to all sites is the negative correlation that G1, the Gender variable, has with the LSIZ scale. Essentially this negative correlation with life satisfaction points out the particular and systematic finding of low morale or life satisfaction for males across all sites. As a variable important across most of the sites HEALTH seems to be a next important finding followed by MASTERY. The sense of MASTERY is important in San Antonio and for the New Mexico sample. ADL or ability to handle the exigencies of daily living is associated positively with life satisfaction only in San Antonio.

Of considerable interest are the findings for the Hartford site for the elderly Puerto Ricans. Given that this is a study of age, the only analysis in which this variable enters the model is for Hartford. This variable correlates positive with life satisfaction. Thus as the person ages higher life satisfaction ensues. This sample group also had the youngest mean age of all the four sites. There are some other patterns that are of interest. The group is influenced by the effects of low income, low levels of education, and the BICUL variable. These three variables have negative zero-order correlations with life satisfaction and are difficult to reconcile. It needs to be pointed out that this sample group was mostly monolingual, with extremely lower educational and income levels attainment than all the site groups. At first glance, the direction of the correlation,

Table 4.
Multiple Regression by Sites

Variable Entered	F Ratio	D/F	Signif. Level	Mult. R	R^2	Zero Correl.
San Antonio						
G1	29.762	1/98	.0000	.4826	.2329	-.636
HEALTH	27.096	2/97	.0000	.5987	.3584	.083
MASTERY	23.623	3/96	.0000	.6516	.4247	.209
ADL	19.593	4/95	.0000	.6723	.4520	.103
Hartford						
G1	97.199	1/103	.0000	.6968	.4855	-.697
HEALTH	54.054	2/102	.0000	.7173	.5145	.248
AGE	40.200	3/101	.0000	.7377	.5442	.109
CA	32.455	4/100	.0000	.7516	.5648	.135
INCOME	28.280	5/99	.0000	.7669	.5882	-.165
BICUL	25.715	6/98	.0000	.7820	.6116	-.011
EDUC	23.417	7/97	.0000	.7926	.6282	-.145
New Mexico						
G1	69.551	1/114	.0000	.6156	.3789	-.616
MASTERY	51.677	2/113	.0000	.6912	.4777	.304
South Texas						
G1	84.689	1/112	.0000	.6562	.4306	-.656

although negative, would seem to indicate that higher income, education, and ability to handle English and Spanish would have a negative effect on life satisfaction. The low correlation negative coefficients for these three variables means a different interpretation of the findings. It could be posited that this group probably had a small number of subjects which had better-than-average education, slightly more income, and were less monolingual. These effects would be sufficient to reverse the direction of the sign of the correlation coefficient. This small incremental change plus the size of the sample would be sufficent to produce a statistical significance. It must be kept in mind that the size of the coefficients is very small. Additionally, this thesis is borne out by noting that the Hartford sample was first generation immi-grants. They were the poorest of all groups, the least educated, and the most monolingual.

In the Hartford sample, the effect of agency participation is also positively correlated with higher life satisfaction. It illustrates the effect of receiving services from a community agency. It graphically illustrates the importance of agency support to the Hispanic elderly in Hartford. This is further borne out by a bivariate analysis using chi-square of the community and agency group cross classified by high and low levels of HEALTH, ADL, and MASTERY in the initial data analysis. All these chi-squares were statistically significant illustrating lower health, activities of daily living, and mastery scores for the agency group as compared to the community group (NHCoA Final Report, 1986).

The data presented in Table 3 explain more of the variance than in the previous analysis. The multiple R squared accounted for sixty-three percent of the variance and included more of the predictor variables than any of the other sites. Does this mean that the regression model with these types of variables predicts more of the variance than for groups less deprived? Obviously more analysis with other deprived groups should add to knowledge in this area. What effects did data collection have on the predictor variables? This data for this site had the least number of missing data for all the cases (NHCoA Final Report, 1986). Were conditions in the data collection interviews different for this group than for the other sites? Did age or other differences in the Hartford sample produce better interviews with less missing data? In all the analyses presented thus far the mean of the variables was used to compensate for missing data even though a judgement was rendered that the number of missing cases per variable was not detrimental to the use of this type of analysis.

Selected Zero-Order Correlations and Life Satisfaction by Site

A number of first-order correlation coefficients which reached statistical significance but in some cases did not enter the multiple regressions are of interest. The following table presents this data. For each site the correlation coefficient, its significance level, and number of cases are presented for each variable and each site.

REL or level of self-perceived religiosity is significant statistically for each of the sites. Since it is a positive correlation, higher level of self-perceived religiosity would be associated with greater life satisfaction. RELPREF, on the other hand, changes direction. This variable, which has a negatively sign for Hartford and for the South Texas sample, indicates that being other than Catholic is associated with higher levels of life satisfaction. The level of significance is not very high, ranging from eleven to twelve percent, but is still highly instructive. Being Catholic, however, seems more important for the San Antonio sample but not for the New Mexico sample. The NHCoA Final Report to the Administration on Aging (AoA) indicates a larger percentage of elderly claiming to be Pentecostals in Hartford. For the South Texas area, a larger

Table 5.
Zero order Correlations and Life Satisfaction By Site

	Rel	Rel Pref	Esteem	Health	Exp	ADL	Educ.
San Antonio							
r	.150	.201	.411	.336	-.069	.334	.227
significant	.068	.023	.000	.000	.247	.000	.012
number	96	95	96	95	96	97	89
Hartford							
r	.378	-.123	.183	.248	.001	.144	.109
significant	000	.106	.031	.005	.497	.022	.175
number	101	99	101	105	101	101	101
New Mexico							
r	.227	.058	.200	.192	-.071	.146	.086
significant	007	.268	.016	.019	.225	.059	.179
number	111	110	108	112	114	113	111
South Texas							
r	.171	-.108	.035	-.035	.040	.056	.09
significant	035	.127	.356	.357	.336	.278	.170
number	99	104	107	101	108	104	106

percentage of Lutherans were reported (NHCoA Final Report, 1986).

High levels of self-esteem indicate its importance for all but the South Texas site. Why these differences are not consistent across all sites is a matter for further conjecture and research. It is to be noted that the value of the correlation reaches .411 between self-esteem and life satisfaction for San Antonio. This is the next highest value to G1 discussed earlier.

Health is a variable that seems more aligned with the urban sample than the rural sample. It is statistically significant at the .01 level for New Mexico in Table 5. As a variable, it does not enter the previous multiple regression models.

A variable that did not enter any of the preceding models is EXP. This variable is a recoding of a variable that attempted to gauge the effects of higher frequencies of visiting and contact with significant others and life satisfaction. As noted, this variable showed little impact.

The patterns of ADL and HEALTH seem parallel. Both variables are similar across sites. It is only for the South Texas sample that both variables are statistically non-significant by the usual definition of significance of .05 values and above. Being able to manage household and social chores is important for most of the Hispanic elderly in this study. The highest health scores for both males and females occur in the South Texas area. Clearly the composite self-rated scores were above the overall group mean for the South Texas group (NHCoA Final Report, 1986). Is health care more readily available in South Texas than in the other areas?

The educational level was important only for the San Antonio group. The value of the correlation coefficient reached .227 and was significant at the .01 level. All the other significant levels were at the .17 level of significance.

Discussion

The premise that life satisfaction should have both program and practice implications is illustrated by some of the findings in the data. The multiple R's are modestly high and point to the type of factors that impinge on a rather poor and deprived segment of the population. Some of the variables that seem to impact across locale were GENDER, HEALTH, and ADL and in some cases MASTERY. These factors should be scrutinized when considering the problem of being at risk for lowered life satisfaction for elderly Hispanics. Some of these variables varied in importance across sites, indicating that one needs to consider regional difference and different histories of the elderly person.

By way of implications, this paper began by raising the question of life satisfaction as both a program-affecting variable and an important factor in clinical work with the Hispanic elderly. It would seem that issues of health, being able to carry out the activities of daily living, would affect the daily lives of these elderly. Further, gender differences were noted ,with the males having lower life satisfaction. Related to this question is the role of psychological coping resources which seemed to be important in the data. Not only is the sense of efficacy as measured by the MASTERY scale important, as the data suggest, but feeling efficacious may also have an effect on feelings of self-worth.

Similarly, the role of religion was examined and found to have important effects on life satisfaction. The need to analyze the relationship between these two variables is a question for future studies. One could posit that organized religion is changing its methods of meeting the social and spiritual needs of elderly Hispanics. This can be seen in the number of converts to religions that make house-calls a practice and provide services in the individual's native tongue. It would seem that different religious groups are serving the Hispanic elderly differently. Perceived life satisfaction would be lower if indeed all social institutions conducted their services in a language that is not easily understood.

It was the intent of this paper to provide clear program and policy implications important in the lives of elderly persons. The need to inform practioners of the implications contained in this study is of vital importance when one is in the field and can readily see the short-comings of the present system of service delivery to the Hispanic elderly. The need to deliver services to Hispanic elderly in a manner that is culturally relevant and that promotes pride and self-esteem is immediate.

One set of findings underscores the importance of support that agencies can give in assisting the elderly person. This one finding illustrates that indeed life satisfaction can be used as a program impact variable. An overview of the findings seems to suggest that for the Hartford sample, difference in life satisfaction may be related to program participation. Attention needs to be paid to the type of participants in programs. Are those who are active partici-pants also higher in life satisfaction or is the program having a positive effect on the person? Studies should be set up to determine the relative effect of program participation on the well-being of elderly. Such studies should evaluate type of program, access to services, and program activities. It would seem that gender differences in social program participation need to be evaluated. Do older Hispanic males have more difficulty participating in age-related social activities? Why were gender differences so pronounced in this data? Are there differences in older Hispanic males in carrying out active roles in which to find self-esteem? This line of reasoning would suggest that role continuity exists for the Hispanic elderly female but not for the male. Women seem to participate in voluntary activities more than men. Programs that provide services to the elderly would do well to consider the male ego when designing recreational and social activities.

The need to provide services in a culturally appropriate manner has been heard over and over again. Programs need to incorporate concepts of reciprocity, *personalismo*, *respeto*, *dignidad* , and *confianza*, and in the language of preference, Spanish or English. There is a need to involve the elderly in all aspects of programing, and to employ them to provide many of these services in their communities. The task is not easy but, as professionals, we should attempt to implement types of programs that will prove to be effective. The goal should be to assist the elderly to attain higher levels of life satisfaction and a sense of control over their lives which will help them live the remainder of their days in dignity.

Despite all the research on the structure of life satisfaction, this analysis can only remain at a crude and global level. Ideally, it would really be of considerable value if predictor variables could be tied to the three specific components of life satisfaction rather than at a second order of abstraction. No theoretical framework has yet been devised that accomplishes this point of specificity. The studies of life satisfaction have come up with different item pools for mood tone, zest versus apathy, and for congruence and fortitude. It would be fruitful to relate subcomponents of the absence of life satisfaction to problems such as depression and the sense that one has little control over one's life. Theory building has not progressed at this level of specificity. It is to be noted that the scale at least is being tested more and more with minority elderly, across gender, and by levels of age.

Coping Styles of Mexican-American Elderly

Hermila Anzaldua, Delores Reed-Sanders,
Robert Wrinkle, and Guadalupe Gibson

My daughter was killed. It was a blow for me, but the Lord
takes over my sufferings and problems. I leave everything to Him.

Mataron a mi hija y fue un golpe muy duro. Pero el Señor se
encarga de mis penas y problemas. Todo se lo dejo a El.

(Mrs. Alcalá, 68 years old, former migrant worker.)

Once out of the hospital, I bought two life insurance policies
to cover all expenses. I informed my oldest son-in-law of arrangements
I had made should anything happen to me. I told him of the
headstone, cemetery lot, and location of all papers.

Una vez salida del hospital, compré dos seguros que
cubrieran ampliamente todo gasto. Hablé con mi yerno mayor, le
informé de mis arreglos si alguna cosa me llegara a pasar. Le informé
de la lápida, lote de cementerio, y lugar donde se encuentran todos
mis documentos.

(Mrs. Moreno, 67 years old, former school cafeteria cook.)

My brother and sister died within the same year. I was un-
able to go to their funerals. It wasn't a problem, it just saddened me.

Mi hermana y hermano murieron el mismo año. No pude ir a sus funerales. No fue problema, nada más me pudo mucho.
(Mr. Alvarado, 79 years old, former construction worker.)

These statements were made by Mexican-American elderly who spoke of the ways they coped with significant life events. The responses illustrate different coping styles to varied life events. Mrs. Alcalá used religiosity to control the stress resulting from the death of her daughter. When Mrs. Moreno was confronted with emergency hospitalization, she used direct action to address the situation by buying life insurance, headstone, and cemetery lot. Mr. Alvarado devalued the relative importance of the deaths of his brother and sister. These varied coping styles reflect the behaviors used to reduce stress from life events.

Review of the Literature
Coping and Events

There has been a great deal of research on the relationship between stressful life events and psychological factors. (See Thotis, 1983 for a review of the literature.) However, the findings suggest weak statistical associations which have directed attention to a more sociological approach to the study of coping and life events. Lazarus, et al. (1974) emphasize that situational variables of coping should be included, but have seldom been more than acknowledged. In their classic study of coping and events, Perlin & Schooler (1978) define coping as behavior in which people engage to avoid being harmed by life strains. People are assumed to respond actively to forces that impinge upon them. In this sense, coping is social in nature and reflects resources which members of society use to understand, adapt, change, or endure the impact of societal forces upon them. They suggest that the protective function of coping behavior is exemplified in three ways: by changing the situation giving rise to the problems, by perceptually changing meaning of the experience to the degree that the problems are neutralized, and by keeping the emotional results of problems within controlled and manageable bounds (Perlin & Schooler, 1978).

Perlin, et al. (1981) examined life events as a part of daily life which differ in number, magnitude, quality, and effects. They suggest that events do not necessarily affect people directly. Life events may create new problems or intensify old ones and call for necessary behaviors with which to cope. Thus, eventful experiences and chronic strains may converge and produce stress.

Life events develop from everyday life situations and are related to normative styles of coping that people learn over time, and share with other group members. Ramos (1979) suggests that we should use the troubles people create for each other in their day-to-day existence to study coping and managing strategies. In this sense, events and coping styles represent the manner in which society and groups influence their members and assume that individuals are participating, active agents who develop coping styles responsive to societal forces.

Mexican-American Elderly

Mexican-Americans constitute the largest Hispanic group in the United States. They reside in every state of the union, including Alaska, but they are highly concentrated in California and Texas.

According to Gelfand (1982), eighty-one percent of Mexican-
Americans live in metropolitan areas. They range from the very poor
to the very rich including some millionaires, but most are
disproportionately poor. Poorest among the Mexican-Americans are
children living in homes headed by women and the elderly.

Many of the elderly are monolingual in Spanish and have
close ties with Mexico. Some came to this country from Mexico as
older people. Others came as children or young adults, while many
are native born. Maldonado (1985) notes that close to fifty percent of
older Mexican-Americans were born in Mexico; therefore, they live
their lives in differing socio-cultural systems. These systems guide
their interactions and provide a spectrum of cultural signatures,
including alternatives with which to cope.

Normative coping styles have been primarily studied using
non-minority group samples (Perlin & Schooler,1978). They note
that the less educated and the poorer elderly are exposed to more
hardships and at the same time are less likely to have the means to
deal with the resulting stresses. Therefore, groups which have
unequal distribution of problems may be similarly unequal in coping
resources. Those who have greater problems may have fewer
resources with which to confront the problems. It may well be that
these groups have developed more clearly refined coping styles to
use their limited resources more efficiently. It may be that these
groups have developed a reservoir of coping styles because they
experience greater negative social forces impacting upon them.
Maldonado (1985) notes that older Hispanics are survivors and their
coping skills and resources should be further studied for possible
policy consideration. Korte (1983) notes the importance of studying

the impact of culture on coping. He laments the fact that social scientists and mental health practitioners have paid little attention to the study of coping styles among Hispanics. In this chapter, we will examine the specific life events confronted by Mexican-American elderly and the array of coping styles developed to address these significant events.

Research Design

The exploratory, qualitative data presented here is a part of a larger study on Hispanic elderly. This part of the study is restricted to Mexican-American elderly. The sample was identified from a random community survey of persons 65 years of age and older who had resided in the United States for a minimum of ten years, and were of low socio-economic status. They lived in the south Texas community of McAllen, located on the Texas-Mexico border. All of the interviews were conducted in Spanish by trained Spanish-speaking interviewers who used an interview schedule which had been back-translated by two of the principal researchers.

The face-to-face interview was oriented toward obtaining several types of information. First, persons were asked to recall a significant life event, either positive or negative, that occurred to them within the last year. The open-ended questions allowed the elderly to choose any event that they felt had made a significant impact upon their lives. Careful attention was given to solicit and record the respondents' exact wording and expressions as they reconstructed the event.

Stressful life events and chronic life strains were differentiated as follows: Stressful life events were considered as discrete happenings restricted in time and place while chronic life strains were perceived as global, continuing happenings which transcended role, time, and place (Krause, 1987). An example of a chronic life strain was a woman's fear that her grandchildren would be harmed. This fear permeated her entire role repertoire. Chronic life strains were not studied.

Life Event Measures

Stressful life events were classified according to the works of Kessler, et al. (1985) and Krause (1987). These researchers suggest that global life-stress indices must be abandoned because diverse types of events are combined into a single unit. Because of their heterogeneity, it is impossible to determine differential impact of a wide range of events. They suggest that researchers should disaggregate global measures into homogeneous specific life-event types. This research sought to classify events into homogeneous groupings by types such as illness, death, or dispute. Events which fell into more than one type were classified according to the most prominent happening. For example, a person may become ill and have a dispute with the spouse concerning expenses. This was classified according to the emphasis of the respondent. If they discussed the illness more than the dispute, it was classified as an illness event. In order to attain a degree of reliability, three coders worked in teams of two on the classification of the events. Working independently, the coders agreed on the categories of 94 percent of the reported events.

Coping Resource Measures

Measurements of coping responses were developed in a similar procedure as life events. In an open-ended interview, respondents were asked a series of questions focusing on how they attempted to deal with the event. The verbatim responses were recorded by the interviewers. Three coders independently classified the coping responses into categories of styles. Respondents were asked a series of questions related to how they addressed the event and attempted to solve the resulting problems. These questions were designed to provide information regarding their coping styles.

Completed interviews were obtained from 88 respondents; 11 interviews were incomplete. The response rate was 88.8%. The respondents were between the ages of 65 and 94 years of age with 38.5% being young-old (65-74), 36.9% being old (75-84), and 24.6% being old-old (85 or older). The majority (61.5%) were female and 38.5% were male. All of them had resided in the United States for at least 10 years. First generation elderly--those not born in the United States--were 53.0% of the sample. The second generation--those born in the United States and who had at least one parent born in Mexico--was 30.3% of the sample. The marital status of respondents was: married (45.3%), widowed (39.1%), divorced or separated (7.8%). In addition, 75% of the respondents had completed four or less years of formal education, 18.8% had completed between five and eight years of formal education, and the remaining 6.8% had no formal education. The level of yearly family income for 86.9% of the sample was less than $6,000. The primary sources of income for 89.3% of the respondents were Social Security and Supplemental Security Income (SSI) with a mean annual income of $3,985. Juárez

(1983) also noted that Mexican-American elderly of South Texas listed their main sources of income as Social Security and SSI and that more than two-thirds were in the low income category ($5,000 or less).

Analysis
A. Events

A series of questions were asked about significant life events. Of the total group 21.6% indicated they had no significant events or stressful happenings during the preceding year. They described how they felt about their lives, degree of contentment, and absence of *mortificaciones* (mortification, humiliation, vexation, or trouble). For example, a 65 year-old farm laborer who had been married to his 49-year-old wife for five years noted that he had no current problems. He stated:

> *We are very contented. Our children and our neighbors visit us. We do favors for others when we can. I have my car; I work; I feel well; I haven't fought with anyone. My health is good. No deaths, no marriages, no one has defrauded me or disappointed me.*

Perlin & Schooler (1978) note that some persons may handle life strains so well that they have no need for coping repertoires. The elderly who reported that no significant event had affected their lives may have prevented hardships from becoming stressful experiences. These cases may illustrate the ultimate in prevention. The remaining elderly related four categories of events which dealt with issues of health, disputes, death, and economics. The most frequently reported events (59.1%) reflected health problems. These encompassed a vast array of illnesses including high blood pressure, diabetes, strokes, heart problems, ulcers, and arthritis. The most frequently appearing health response (19.5%) was in the general category of "illness," without a specific disease or condition either understood or related.

Juárez (1983) noted that Mexican-American elderly most frequently reported arthritis as the disease which had been diagnosed by a physician. Other illnesses reported were high blood pressure, heart conditions, diabetes, and visual/hearing difficulties. Our findings suggest a similar distribution of illnesses.

Events related to disputes among family members, neighbors, or agencies were described by 21.2% of the elderly. The disputes were within the family, primarily with children and grandchildren. Only one respondent, a 66-year-old woman, reported a dispute with a spouse. While he was drinking with friends, he struck her. She became very angry and sprayed him with insecticide. She said, "*I struck him, leaving him with swollen lips, and threw him out.*" This was the only event of spouse abuse which was mutual abuse with the female in both roles of perpetrator and victim.

Other events included a daughter who was pregnant with her eighth child, a daughter who had left school, and a daughter who had suddenly married at age 40 and left the mother feeling abandoned. Grandchildren presented problems such as not working, drinking, and eloping. Neighbor disputes were less frequent and dealt with complaints about dogs and noise. One respondent's neighbor had called the police and complained that she (the respondent) was "crazy." An agency dispute involved the Social Security Office in an alleged over-payment.

Death was the topic of 15.2% of the events. The deaths concerned a wife, a grandson, a mother, a brother, a sister, a daughter, and a niece. It should be emphasized that the sample was restricted to low socio-economic status elderly who currently and throughout their life cycle had experienced severe economic problems. They lived in a geographical area with the lowest per capita income of any area in the United States. Juárez (1983) noted that in the midst of these chronic life conditions, the elderly are also affected by the deteriorating economy in Mexico that has resulted in unprecedented devaluations of the peso. Economic events referred to the effects of the peso devaluation upon the lives of a son and a daughter. Another event involved a broken down truck. A surprising finding was that economic events were reported so infrequently. This would suggest that the economic hardships may have become such a pervasive condition over such long periods of time that they were no longer viewed as significant events, but rather as chronic life strains which permeated all facets of their lives.

Females tended to report health-related events, while males tended to report non-health events. Females tended to relate events concerning health and economics while males related events regarding death and disputes. These findings are consistent with those of Juárez (1983) who noted that when comparing Mexican-American and Anglo elderly, the Mexican-American group had considerably poorer health status and experienced more severe economic conditions. When examining Mexican-American males and females, the females were in more difficult conditions than their male counterparts. Our female respondents reported more health and economic events; thus, the significance of the factors on the lives of

Mexican-American elderly females were reemphasized.

B. Social Group

The events were classified according to the social group in which they occurred. Krause (1986) used the classifications of bereavement, crime, network crisis, and financial stressors to examine the relative amounts of stress. This classification scheme combined two criteria; the nature of the event, such as crime and bereavement, and the social group in which the event occurred, such as network crisis which was identified as events involving the respondent's family members or friends. This research used two mutually exclusive categories for events--the nature of the event and the social group in which the event occurred.

The largest proportion of events (35.7%) involved only the respondent. For example, the respondent may have become ill, had an accident and broke her knee, or was devastated when a truck broke down. The event focused on the individual. The second largest social category was that of their children (20.0%), and 15.7% indicated the spouse as the social group category. Extended family included grandchildren, nieces, and nephews and accounted for 15.7% of the responses. Other social groups also included siblings (7.1%), friends and neighbors (2.9%), parents (1.4%) and agencies (1.4%). These findings suggest that the Mexican-American elderly experience significant events of a health nature which primarily concern themselves., and are significantly affected by their own health status. Because only 45.3% of the respondents were currently married, the concern for self may be a function of marital status.

C. Coping Function by Coping Style

Respondents were asked a series of questions concerning how they dealt with the significant events which they related. Following the model of Perlin & Schooler (1978), three functions of coping were identified: the coping response which addressed the situation and attempted to modify it; the coping response which addressed the meaning and attempted to control it; the coping response which addressed the stress.

There were 66 respondents who reported a coping style related to a significant event in their lives during the past 12 months. As noted in Table 1, the coping function which was most frequently reported (59.1%) was controlling stress. These elderly dealt with events by attempting to control the stress with a wide array of coping styles. Religiosity (30.8%), helplessness (28.2%), passive acceptance (15.4%), and resignation (12.8%) were the most frequently reported coping styles directed toward controlling stress. Coping styles which attempted to modify the situation were used by 30.3% of the respondents. The coping styles within this category included direct action (45.0%), seek help (30.0%), and mobilize support (15.0%). The least frequent coping function was directed at controlling the meaning of stressful events (10.6%). The coping styles for this function were devaluation of importance (57.1%), selective ignoring (28.6%) and hierarchical ordering (14.3%). Mexican-American elderly addressed significant life events with a rich repertoire of coping styles which focused primarily on controlling stress; however, they possessed a wide range of styles which served to address eventful stresses.

Table 1

Frequency of types of coping functions for selected coping styles among Mexican-American elderly

| | Coping Functions | | | | | |
Selected Coping Styles	Control Stress F	%	Modify Situation F	%	Control Meaning F	%
Religiosity	12	(30.8%)				
Helplessness	11	(28.2%)				
Passive Acceptance	6	(15.4%)				
Resignation	5	(12.8%)				
Withdrawal	3	(7.7%)				
Control Anger	1	(2.6%)				
Folk Wisdom	1	(2.6%)				
Direct Action			9	(45.0%)		
Seek Help			6	(30.0%)		
Mobilize Support			3	(15.0%)		
Give Help			1	(5.0%)		
Communication			1	(5.0%)		
Devaluation of Importance					4	(57.1%)
Selective Ignoring					2	(28.6%)
Hierarchical Order					1	(14.3%)
Totals	39	(100%)	20	(100%)	7	(100%)

Examples of Coping Styles to Control Stress
A. Religiosity

Mrs. Gonzalez is an 82-year-old widow whose vision and
ability to walk were impaired. SS provided her a $4,200 annual
income. She talked of being fearful when her son informed her that
he would undergo a second heart surgery immediately. She
composed herself, gave her son her blessing, and entrusted him to
the "Lord's care." She related:

> *I thought, would he live or not? I would pray and thought of
> his children who needed him. I asked God to let him live for
> the sake of his children who had no one else but him. I felt I
> couldn't handle it without God's help. I couldn't go to
> Houston because of my leg; so, I stayed here, praying for him
> and turning him over to God. El (Dios) sabe lo que hace.*

B. Helplessness

Mr. Ayala was an 83-year-old widower whose six children
lived close to him in neighboring communities. He was monolingual
in Spanish with no formal education. His income, derived from
Social Security and SSI, amounts to $4,100 per year. In months past
he had received a letter from the Social Security Office advising him
that he had received and cashed a $120 check issued to him in error.
Mr. Ayala was in tears when he told the interviewer his detailed
event. He related in emotional terms:

> *They sent me a letter charging me $120 which had been sent
> to me by mistake. I now had to reimburse this. Señorita, I
> swear before God that I never received the money. I have
> just received my usual two checks. I was very hurt and I felt*

badly because I was blamed without reason. Even now I feel badly. It embarrasses me that they think I have done this. They say they will send someone to my home to investigate further. It will embarrass me greatly if they tell the people at the grocery store about this. Sometimes I cannot sleep wondering how I am going to resolve this. They asked me to come to the agency and they told me they would send an investigator to check everything in my home. What will they do with me? Not having anyone to defend me or listen to me I feel defenseless before the government and educated people. I feel I have been condemned unjustly. I feel like a fugitive who has not been given a chance. Me siento con una condena sin justicia; como prófugo que no le han dado chance de defenderse y asi ya lo han hallado culpable.

C. Passive Acceptance

Mr. Aguirre was an 82-year-old married father of four children who lived in the area. He was a farm laborer, currently retired, with a total annual income from Social Security and SSI in the amount of $6,000. He completed a third grade education in Mexico. His significant event concerned his own hospitalization because of prostate and bladder problems. Mr Aguirre told of initially reacting with fear and sadness when he was given his diagnosis. As he told of his experience, he described how his apprehension gave way to passive acceptance:

When they explained my illness I was saddened, felt a knot in my throat, and felt like crying. I speculated my illness was terminal. I felt unable to surmount my fear. In time I realized this was my destiny but I had to make the effort to live longer. In order to do that I would have to follow the doctor's instructions, take my medication and rest a lot. I felt God gave me this destiny and I accepted it.

D. Resignation

Seventy-seven-year-old Mr. Alvarez referred to his wife's death and how it affected him. Mr. Alvarez had a fourth-grade education and worked most of his life as a public school janitor. He had six children, all of whom are married and live out of the state. Social Security provides him an annual pension of $3,000 and this is his only source of income. His wife died from diabetic complications and a sudden heart attack. Mr. Aguirre recalled that his wife anticipated her death because she was always admonishing him to remember "to do this and that" after she died. Mr. Aguirre wept as he talked of having to endure and go on because that is how God wanted it. He described the "aching" in his heart as a *pena moral* .

When we arrived at the hospital I was terrified. I didn't know what to think. While they examined her I called my daughter who was then living in San Juan, Texas. I felt very alone and started to cry. My daughter arrived and then the doctor told us he could do no more, that she was in God's hands. My children helped me a lot. Without them I could not have gone through it all. They gave me strength and I supported them. I tried to be resigned and not cause them further grief.

E. Modify Situation
1. Direct Action

Mrs. Salas was an 80-year-old widow with three children who lived alone and had no formal education. Her social security and SSI provide an annual income of $2,100. The highest income she ever received was $3,000. The family dispute which she related was:

> My dead daughter's children and their father lived with me. I told them they could no longer live with me because I could not take care of them because of my illness. I told them to go live with their sister because I was ill and I couldn't wash so many men's clothes and do heavy ironing. They were hurt. I was very sorry. "Se me partía el alma." But I could no longer carry the load. I felt badly and I didn't want God to punish me, but I don't think He will. Although I may seem egotistical, now I can sleep well, eat well ,and don't worry. I feel more at ease. It was too much "mortificación" when they went out or went with the fellow next door to drink beer.

Another illustration of the direct action coping style is the case of Mrs. Garza. She was a 66-year-old woman with three years of formal education and an annual income of $1,400. She never worked outside the home. She could not see well and the neighborhood children threw rocks at her. "No miro muy bien, y los muchachos me apedrean." She had no children, nieces or nephews, or compadres. Her significant event was a dispute with the man with whom she lived. She stated:

> He (spouse) was in a hotel with another woman when he heard I was ill. I got angry. I came to my house where he

> *drank with friends. He was eating. I sprayed him with*
> *insecticide. I struck him, leaving him with swelled lips and*
> *threw him out and continued to strike him.*

She took the situation into her own hands with apparent self-assertion.

2. Seek Help

Mr. Rodriguez was 84 years old, married, and lived with his wife in the family home where they had resided for 43 years. He was monolingual in Spanish with no formal education, retired, and disabled. Before retirement Mr. Rodriguez was a migrant farm worker whose highest salary ever received was $3,000. SSI is his only income. He was born in Mexico and came to this area as a young man. Mr. Rodriguez' significant event concerned his diabetic son:

> *My son, Santos, came to visit us on his birthday. He hurt an*
> *already injured foot that became worse due to his diabetes.*
> *The foot became infected and it had to be amputated. We*
> *took him to a Reynosa (Mexico) doctor. He immediately told*
> *us that he had to amputate the foot. I felt I needed to be*
> *strong in order to help my son go through all of this. He did*
> *not vacillate nor become childish (achicaparo) in taking care*
> *of himself because of his many children. I took him to the*
> *doctor and I called his "patrón " who authorized his care and*
> *said he would pay.*

3. Mobilize Support

Mrs. Gutierrez was 65 years of age and lived with her husband of 43 years. She had no formal education, and her annual income of Social Security and SSI was $5,000. Five of their seven children lived near her, and the others lived in other Texas communities. Her husband became ill and this event significantly affected her life. Her coping style was to mobilize support. She stated:

> *One night he worsened. I called the children to take us to the hospital. Some of the children called others. We all arrived at the hospital and started praying while he was being attended. Everyone in the family went. I could not have done it alone. I don't know English and had no transportation. Therefore, it was difficult, but I wrestled with it. "Pero le hice la lucha."*

Mrs. Gutierrez graphically illustrated how she mobilized support to address the problem. Her coping style was diametrically opposed to withdrawal, passive acceptance, or helplessness.

F. Control Meaning
Devaluation of Importance

Mrs. Díaz was an 83-year-old, married woman who lived with her husband. They had been married 51 years. She had a third-grade level of formal education, was monolingual in Spanish, and had worked as a packer in produce sheds. Her family income was $3,000 per year derived from Social Security and SSI. She had five children who lived near her. The illness of her 89-year-old husband significantly affected her life. Mr. Díaz was hospitalized for five days because of a blood clot. She coped with this situation by devaluating the importance of the illness. She stated:

When they called me, I was frightened, but I controlled myself because the doctor had told me not to worry about anything since I could have another stroke. I tried to calm my children saying they should thank God that He had left him for so many years. That is what is important. But "ni modo".

Summary and Conclusions

This exploratory study focused on issues of significant events and coping styles of a random sample of 88 Mexican-American elderly who lived in South Texas near the Texas-Mexico border. They were between the ages of 65 and 94, of low socio-economic status, and had lived in the United States for at least 10 years. The majority were female, had completed four or less years of formal education, and received an annual family income of less than $5,000. The primary sources of income were Social Security and Supple-mental Security Income.

Approximately one-fifth of the elderly reported no significant event or stressful happening during the preceding year. They may represent the ultimate in coping efficacy because they handle events by not allowing them to become a problem. The remaining elderly related events concerning health, dispute, death, and economics. Health issues were the most frequently reported and reflected the critical health status of Mexican-American elderly.

Coping styles may have the function of controlling stress, modifying the situation, or controlling the meaning of the stressful event. The elderly most frequently addressed stressful events by controlling stress through the coping styles of religiosity, helpless-ness, passive acceptance, and resignation. There was a tendency to use the control stress function regardless of the type of event faced. Mexican-American elderly also coped with stress by attempting to modify the situation with the styles of direct action, giving and seeking help, and mobilizing support. To a lesser extent, the respondents sought to control the meaning of the significant events with the coping styles of devaluation of importance and selective ignoring.

Perlin & Schooler (1978) used an urban Chicago sample, between the ages of 18 and 65, to examine the relative effectiveness of the psychological resources and coping responses within four roles. They found that the better educated and more economically affluent group tended to have more effective coping responses while the less educated and poor had fewer means to deal with role strains and stresses. Their respondents primarily used the coping function of meaning control, while our sample tended to use stress control most often. The relative powerlessness of the elderly may explain the reliance upon stress control in an effort to accommodate to conditions that cannot be changed. Our study examined a single coping style focused on a single event while Perlin & Schooler focused on an array of responses within the roles of parents, spouse, occupation, and economics. They found that no single coping response appeared as effective as having a variety of responses. Self-concept may affect coping mechanisms. In addition, a single individual may use an array of coping styles. Our study did not address these issues. With this caveat, our study does suggest that Mexican-American elderly have a range of coping styles with which to address significant life events effectively under extreme social conditions. They truly are survivors. These strengths are noteworthy and should be further studied and considered in terms of public policy.

Religiosity as a Coping Mechanism Among Hispanic Elderly

Daniel T. Gallego

Anthropologists tell us that religion plays a very important role in the lives of human beings. From the beginning of recorded history, drawings and pictographs have been found that help us understand how ancient men and women coped with uncertainties and severe environmental conditions.

Religious beliefs and rituals help us to make life bearable by explaining the unexplainable. Questions arising from the loss of a spouse, loss of youthfulness or health, the seemingly harsh environmental conditions, and trials that the elderly must go through can partially be answered and explained by religion.

Religion enhances our self-importance and makes us feel that we are not creations of an unplanned, chaotic universe but rather we are part of a cosmic plan that is orderly and in which we have a very important role to play--we are children of God. If we are children of God, then we are important because we come from a royal lineage. In later years, religion helps the objective self, the "me," in understanding what we think and feel about ourselves. If we look at the four components in the development of self-esteem, *self-concept, ideal self, self-evaluation,* and finally *self-esteem*, we find that religion plays a very important role in determining what the ideal self is supposed to be. This certainly affects the self-evaluation of the person and ultimately the self-esteem of that person, if religion plays an important part in his/her life.

Without religion there would be no order in society, because religion sanctions the local norms of that society. If a man/woman will not sin against God, he/she will not sin against the children of God. We don't run stop signs because God doesn't want us to, for in so doing, we might hurt one of His children. An American dissident who was living in Guadalajara, Mexico, once said to the author as he contemplated the absence of crime in his neighborhood ,

> *Religion...I don't personally believe in a God...but if there would be no God...I would create one and I would make him kind, loving, and understanding so that people would want to be like him. I would also make him strict and stern with his children, to have them understand that order is a must in his domain. I would give him whatever attributes people envision God to have.*

Once this God is created and his explanations for an unbearable world are set in motion, the next task is to indoctrinate these human beings to believe that such a person exists and that everything we do is related to this personal God. Elderly people who are children of God don't commit suicide because God doesn't believe in suicide. Elderly people who are religious and believe in God are not supposed to get depressed, because they are important. Elderly people who are religious adapt to aging and the losses that come with aging because they see the total scheme and plan of life. Elderly people who are religious---and the list of rationalizations goes on to create an asymmetrical relationship between religion and coping mechanisms.

It is an impossibility to understand a culture or an ethnic subgroup without understanding what their beliefs are about the supernatural, the legends, and the myths that are all tied into a bundle called religion.

Historical Antecedents to Present-Day Religious Behavior

In addition to the above mentioned functions which religion serves for individual needs, it has yet a broader function that it serves for society. That function is to socialize the individual into a way of thinking that is consistent with the society from whence it developed. The ultimate objective of the larger institution that represents all churches and denominations which are institutional agents is that of assimilation. In the case of the American society, there is a strong drive towards Americanization. There is a difference between Spanish Catholicism and American Catholicism, between European Protestantism and American Protestantism. The differences have developed as a result of evolution as the institution of religion has attempted to integrate itself with the other institutions, economic, educational, political, and the family. The role of religion as a teacher of societal values and norms is either enhanced or hindered by any one of the following factors:

1. The attitudes of the majority group;
2. The attitudes of the minority group;
3. The cultural kinship, which includes such factors as religion, language similarities, and values of the culture;
4. The race of the persons being taught;

5. The relative size of the groups involved;
6. The manner of settlement, whether rural or urban, and the extent of its isolation;
7. The age and sex composition of the group

(Berry & Tischler, 1978).

The Hispanic population in the United States has been a challenge to religious institutions who have attempted to inculcate the American norms and values into an ethnic group that is well entrenched in Spanish-Indian traditions. The Latino has in the past possessed every characteristic that would hinder the process of Americanization. In many ways the tendency of the Hispanic in America has always been toward voluntary segregation because of the relative small number of groups involved and reluctance to become "americanized". Culturally, the Hispanic is very different from the North Western European whose heritage is dominant in America. The New World Hispanic is different in color, language, value system, and religion. The efforts of the American Catholic Church and the Protestant Churches to Americanize the sizeable Hispanic population in America has been frustrating, to say the least.

Both the Catholics and the Protestants inherited the problems that the Spanish Catholics had with the New World Hispanics. Those problems dealt with:

1. The diversity of the indigenous Indian populations.
2. The lack of resources of the population to support the church.
3. In the case of Mexico and South America, the immense distance between populated centers.

4. The "pagan" religious orientations of the New World people.

These problems have prompted Catholic and Protestant churches to react with programs that have, in the long run, affected church affiliation, church attendance, and the degree of religiosity among Hispanics in the New World.

The first approach used by both Catholic and Protestant churches in servicing the needs of the Hispanic is that of providing "religious care" as the primary mandate of the churches. This approach saw and treated the Hispanic natives as pagans who needed to be converted to Christianity. This conservative tradition required the "client" to become totally immersed in the values of the institution (Castañeda,1936). This approach also viewed the client as incapable of being immersed into the structure of the church. The clergy was selected from members of the dominant society or from members of European countries that understood the language but not the customs of the people they were servicing. The pastoral orientation of the Catholic Church saw the "padre" on horseback with his saddlebags full of a Mass kit, holy oils, a rosary, and catechism, saying Mass in every home where he stopped for water or nourishment. He performed marriages for those living in sin, instructed, brought comfort to the sick and afflicted, and provided the religious essentials that a padre was trained to do in seminary (Castañeda, 1936). For the Protestants, Melinda Rankin, Vernon McCombs, and "Mexican" Brown were all catalysts in getting the evangelical work started for the Presbyterians, Methodists, and Baptists (Grebler, More & Guzman, 1970). For most of the Protestant evangelists, the Mexicans were defined as pagans. One of the reasons why they became involved in proselyting work among the Mexicans was to combat the Catholic presence in all of the Southwest (Rankin, 1960).

The pastoral approach used by the American churches failed among the Hispanics because of lack of resources by the parent churches and failure of Hispanics to support the evangelical movement.

The second approach used by religious institutions in America, both Catholic and Protestant, was that of adopting a secular mission to Americanize the New World Hispanics. This was in hopes that by becoming mainstream Americans, the value systems, educational levels, and socio-economic statuses would all improve, and then the Hispanics would be more immersed in the doctrines of the church (Grebler, Moore and Guzman, 1970). This approach saw the need, first of all, of bringing the malnourished child up to an acceptable level of health, and then having that child make the contributions necessary to take care of self and the church. This liberal position maintained that the institution was there to service individual members, to help them become healthy. It ranged from evangelical paternalism to self-determination, from strict adherence of the client to values of the religion, to the nurturing of clients through assistance in their non-institutional role. This new approach saw the church as a means rather than as an end in itself.

When the second approach was adopted, the Catholic Church in the West moved from a pastoral church to a social action church, which involved alliances with labor unions and community programs to bring the malnourished child back to health. The Protestant church likewise moved very strongly from evangelical work to social action, settlement house approaches, all aimed at helping the process of Americanization to take hold in the lives of the Hispanic (National Council of Churches, 1956-1958).

One problem has always existed among the approaches used by the American churches--the problem of segregation and separation of the Hispanic congregations from the Anglo congregations. This separation arose because of differences in race, color, socio-economic status, language barriers, prejudices on the part of both the Hispanic and the majority group, and a multitude of other factors. Voluntary or involuntary--it really doesn't make any difference. If the main objective of the church was to Americanize the Hispanic into the dominant culture, it has failed.

Church affiliation, church attendance, ideological beliefs in religious doctrine, and the role that these beliefs have in helping the individual cope with the stresses of the world are all dependent on the following variables.

1. How the religion was introduced to the culture.
2. The involvement of the people in creating culturally relevant rituals that exemplify their beliefs.
3. The educational level of the people being indoctrinated.
4. The behavior of the clergy in teaching the religious doctrine.
5. The lack of resources of the people being served.
6. The Americanization of a religion.
7. The role of the church in solving worldly problem through social action.

Religious Characteristics of the Sample
A. Religious Preference

One of the commonalities that all Hispanic elderly have, whether they are Cuban, Puerto Rican, South American, Central American, Mexican, or Mexican-American in origin, is that somewhere back in their family history, either they or their parents were Catholic in religious affiliation. The religious preference of individuals participating in this research project suggests that in the last 20 years or so the number of Hispanics who list themselves as Protestants has grown from approximately 5 percent to 18 percent. Eighty-two percent of the sample declared themselves to be Catholic and 18 percent listed themselves as Protestant. The percentage of Catholics was higher in New Mexico where 92 percent of the sample declared Catholicism as their religious preference as compared to South Texas which only claimed 78 percent Catholic. When religious preference was cross-tabulated with the sites of the sample, it was found that there was a significant relationship between the two variables, as indicated by a chi-square of 38.865 with 15 degrees of freedom.

Almost 85 percent of the sample claimed some church membership, with San Antonio, Texas, New Mexico, and South Texas respondents having the highest declaration (from 88 percent to 90 percent) of church membership. The sample from Hartford claimed only 70 percent membership in any religious organization. The relationship between church membership and site of the sample also was significant at the .01 level with a chi-square of 16.315, as illustrated in Table 1.

Table 1
Religious Preference by Samplig Area
By Frequency and Percentage

Sampling Area	Catholic		Protestant		Other		Total	
	No.	%	No.	%	No.	%	No.	%
San Antonio	84	29.6	8	18.6	5	31.3	97	28.3
Hartford	62	21.8	18	41.9	5	31.3	85	24.8
New Mexico	72	25.3	2	4.7	0	0	74	21.6
South Texas	66	23.2	15	34.8	6	37.4	87	25.3
Total	284	100	43	100	16	100	N=343	100

These gross percentages overlook an important variable that must be recognized when looking at church membership and a variable that was not obtained in the collection of data. Obviously there are different types of members in any one religious group, just as there are multitudes of reasons why those individuals joined the church. Vernon (1962), for example, in his study of religious preference, distinguished what he called

1. dormant Catholics,
2. marginal Catholics,
3. nominal Catholics, and
4. nuclear Catholics.

Others like Ringer, Luckman and Spitzer followed similar patterns of identifying different types of members (Glock,1960).

Table 2
Church Membership by Sampling Area
By Frequency and Percentage

	Yes		No		Total	
	No	%	No	%	No	%
San Antonio	64	32.0	8	22.2	72	30.5
Hartford	39	19.5	17	47.2	56	23.7
New Mexico	48	24.0	5	13.9	53	22.5
South Texas	49	24.5	6	16.7	55	23.3
Total	200	100	36	100	N=236	100

B. Church Attendance

The respondents in this sample were asked the question, "Do you attend services more or less than you did at age 55?" Both males and females in the sample responded that they attended services less than they did when they were 55 years old. Almost 50 percent of the sample indicated that they participated less, 29 percent indicated that it was about the same, and almost 21 percent indicated that they attended services more. When compared to the dominant society, this statistic is in line with the role changes that occur as one grows older. There is an overall decline in participation in voluntary associations in terms of number of memberships held as well as number of meetings attended. Factors that generally affect the participation level of the elderly are:

1. The social class of the individual--lower class people are

less likely to participate in voluntary organizations than middle or upper class individuals;

2. The degree of independence or dependence-- dependent persons hold a status very similar to children. Society expects them to defer gratification to their benefactors, to be grateful for what they receive, and to give up the right to self-determination;

3. Disability and sickness--over a third of the elderly in our society have a disability that limits them to activities around the house (Wilder & Niven, 1958).

Men were less likely to attend church than women. As high as 28 percent of the men never attended church and, when combined with those that attended once a month, this statistic amounted to almost 50 percent of the male population. The reasons given by

Table 3
Church Attendance by Sample Area
By Frequency and Percentage

	Never		Once Month		Less than Month		Weekly		Twice Week		Daily		Total	
	No	%	No	%	No	%	No	%	No	%	No	%	No	%
San Antonio	12	20.0	13	31.0	6	11.6	46	32.2	8	22.2	8	53.4	93	26.8
Hartford	25	41.7	10	23.8	18	35.3	14	9.7	16	44.4	2	13.3	85	24.5
New Mexico	5	8.3	6	14.2	16	31.3	40	28.0	8	22.2	3	20.0	78	22.5
South Texas	18	30.0	13	31.0	11	21.6	43	30.1	4	11.2	2	13.3	91	26.2
Total	60	100	42	100	51	100	143	100	36	100	15	100	N=347	100

Table 4
Reasons for Non-attendance to Church by Sampling Area
By Frequency and Percentage

Sampling Area	No Trans-portation		Physical Problems		Other		Total	
	No	%	No	%	No	%	No	%
San Antonio	6	14.3	30	29.7	2	6.1	38	21.6
Hartford	9	21.4	35	34.7	10	30.2	54	30.7
New Mexico	14	33.3	15	14.9	2	6.1	31	17.6
South Texas	13	31.0	21	20.7	19	57.6	53	30.1
Total	42	100	101	100	33	100	N=176	100

males for non-attendance were "no transportation" and "major physical problems." These two reasons accounted for almost 45 percent of the non-attendance among men.

Forty-one percent of the women attended church less than once a month with 12 percent never attending church at all. This study suggests that women are more likely to attend church than their counterparts, the men, whose attendance is not regular. Reasons given by the women for not attending church coincided with those given by the men.

Church attendance figures seem to be an important criteria to take into consideration when looking at the role that religion plays in the life of the respondent. However, it should be recognized that there are many reasons for attending or for not attending church. Some elderly may attend because they define church attendance as a duty and obligation. Others may attend church because of habit, or it may provide the worshipper with the sense of receiving spiritual help. There are probably as many different reasons for attending church as there are for not attending church. The point that is being made is that looking at church attendance does not measure, in the last analysis, whether the individual is spiritually religious or otherwise.

C. Religious Programming

The non-attendance of church does not mean that individuals are not receiving religious instruction or having their religious needs met. As high as 75 percent of the sample listened to religious programming of some sort, i.e., via radio or television. An interesting phenomenon is that even though the Hartford sample had the lowest declared religious affiliation preference, it had the highest percentage (89 percent) of respondents who listened to religious programming. (See Table 5).

Table 5
Listens to Services on Radio or Television
By Frequency and Percentage

Sampling Area	Yes		No		Total	
	No	%	No	%	No	%
San Antonio	64	24.3	28	34.6	92	26.7
Hartford	75	28.5	8	9.9	83	24.1
New Mexico	48	18.3	30	37.0	78	22.7
South Texas	76	28.9	15	18.5	91	26.5
Total	263	100	81	100	N=344	100

D. Faith

The respondents in the study were asked the question, "Do you believe that faith can help a person dealing with life's problems?" Ninety-three percent of the respondents answered in the positive. The question did not specifically identify who the individuals were supposed to have faith in to help deal with their problems--whether in themselves, God, or fate. (See Table 6).

Table 6
Belief in Faith by Sampling Area
By Frequency and Percentage

Sampling Area	Yes No	Yes %	No No	No %	Total No	Total %
San Antonio	89	27.1	3	27.3	92	27.1
Hartford	84	25.6	1	9.1	85	25.1
New Mexico	71	21.6	5	45.5	76	22.4
South Texas	84	25.6	2	18.1	86	25.4
Total	328	100	11	100	N=339	100

The Concept of Religiosity

The concept of "religiosity" is generally used to describe a whole configuration of behavior patterns, including feelings, attitudes, and emotions, all of which are presumably summated and responded to an entity. The term is a troublesome and amorphous one and possibly might lack validity because of the broad, encompassing area that it is trying to measure. The term is supposed to measure church membership, church attendance, acceptance of specific beliefs, ideology, and the strength/weakness of belief. All of these variables, put together, are supposed to determine the role that religion plays in the life of an individual. Feifel (1959) has challenged the validity of the term by saying:

> Individuals may derive values (sociability, emotional support, sense of belonging, etc.) and need satisfactions from religious membership and participation that are not necessarily related to religious beliefs and commitment. Also individuals may frequently express a religious identification (tradition) without formal membership or commitment. And often there may be a difference between the value commitment of the individual and those required by the "official" theological structure of his particular faith. In other words, some people may profess religious tenets but not practice them. Others may adopt religion as a kind of defense against the 'slings and arrows of outrageous fortune.' Then, there are those who incorporate their religious beliefs into the activities of everyday living."

The approach that this study has used to determine religiosity is merely to ask the respondents a question as to how interested they are in religion or how important they feel religion to be in their lives. The specific question asked was, "How do you see yourself in relation to religion?" The possible answers that the respondent could have chosen are:

1. quite religious,
2. religious like other people,
3. a little religious,
4. not religious,

5. against religion. (See Table 7).

Table 7
Religiosity by Sampling Area
By Frequency and Percentage

Sampling Area	Not Religious		Little Religious				Average Religious		Quite		Total	
	No	%	No	%	No	%	No	%	No	%		
San Antonio	7	38.9	15	25.4	40	26.1	36	29.3	98	27.8		
Hartford	0	00.0	9	15.3	28	18.3	48	39.0	85	24.1		
New Mexico	4	22.2	14	23.7	42	27.5	18	14.6	78	22.1		
South Texas	7	38.9	21	35.6	43	28.1	21	17.1	92	26.0		
Total	18	100	59	100	153	100	123	100				
									N=353	100		

The data suggests that females considered themselves more "religious" than males. Forty-one percent of the females indicated that they were quite religious, compared to 23 percent of the males who answered that they were quite religious. Forty-three percent of both males and females answered that they were "religious like other people." How the respondents viewed other people's religiosity and religious involvement would certainly vary, thereby yielding differences in interpretation of this question. Twenty-four percent of the male respondents indicated that they were "a little religious" as compared to 13 percent of the female respondents.

Although the percentages seem to suggest that females are more "religious" than males, the way the question was asked might cause the researcher to question whether we can measure the

Table 8
Attendance of Church Services in Comparison to Youth by Sampling Area By Frequency and Percentage

Sampling Area	More Now		About Same		Less Now		Total	
	No	%	No	%	No	%	No	%
San Antonio	22	31.9	30	30.9	39	22.2	91	26.6
Hartford	7	10.1	21	21.6	56	31.8	34	24.6
New Mexico	17	24.6	28	28.9	32	18.2	77	22.5
South Texas	23	33.4	18	18.6	49	27.8	90	26.3
Total	69	100	97	100	176	100	N=342	100

degree of religiosity by asking one question and getting a self-measurement of strength of religious commitment. (See Table 8).

Allport (1960), in his study entiled, *Religion in the Developing Personality*, suggests that there are two kinds of "religiosity":

1.. Religiosity that is strictly utilitarian, self-serving, conferring safety, status, comfort and talismanic favors upon the believer. "God is concerned exclusively with my group, my church, my formula for living." People who are religious in this sense make use of God. In theological terms, they turn to God without turning away from self.

2. Religiosity where religion is seen not as an extrinsic, self-serving value, but rather an intrinsic value, larger than self, wholly beyond self. This kind of religion can stir one's existence without enslaving him to his limited concepts and egocentric needs.

wholly beyond self. This kind of religion can stir one's existence without enslaving him to his limited concepts and egocentric needs.

Allport (1960) suggests that possibly people who break down, who profess a religion, formal or personal, are those for whom religion has an extrinsic but not an intrinsic significance. Or it may turn out that the extrinsic type is well able to hold onto a minimum type of stability, much as do individuals who have strong ego defenses, whereas only the intrinsic type achieves a fully positive mental health. Identification of individuals into either one of these two types of religiosity may provide some important information on how individuals cope with life's stresses.

Religiosity as a Coping Mechanism

If another scale had been used to measure the religiosity of the respondents, and the determination of whether or not the individual was using religion as an intrinsic (larger than self) or an extrinsic (self-serving) value, we might have found that there was an asymmetrical relationship between religiosity, life satisfaction, and mastery. However, this question was not answered because there was only one question used to determine the measure of "religiosity." This measure looked only at the respondents' answer to a rather ambiguous question as to their relation to religion. Nevertheless, when this question was dichotomized into religious and non-religious, and then cross-tabulated against the life satisfaction scale, the self-esteem scale, and the mastery scale, there was no statistical relationships between the variables. Again, this does not mean that there was not a relationship; what it means is that the question that was asked to measure religiosity did not measure religiosity but might have measured church attendance.

Summary and Conclusions

If we look at the functions that the religious institution is supposed to provide for society, we note that most of them deal with explaining the unexplainable. Religious beliefs help humans make life bearable, determining their relationship to the supernatural, to the environment, to time, to activity, and enhancing their self-worth. We cannot understand their rationale until we understand their beliefs in the supernatural.

In addition, religion serves as a socializing agent for assimilating newcomers into a new culture by teaching them the social sanctions of that culture. The Hispanics in the United States have been a challenge to the organized religious agents, both in the Catholic and Protestant groupings. They have been a problem because of their lack of financial resources to support the churches, the refusal of the dominant society to assimilate Hispanic cultural traits into the American religious culture, and finally, because of the historical antecedents that the Hispanics brought with them from the Spanish Catholic Church.

A Preliminary Review of Caregiving Issues and the Hispanic Family

Marta Sotomayor and Suzanne Randolph

Introduction

Among the many factors that hinder the access to and utilization of human and health care services by the Hispanic elderly, none seem as important to the elderly themselves as the perceived insensitivity of such services. Yet, such insensitivity seems to be perpetuated by limited information about cultural and linguistic factors that are separate and apart from issues of poverty. Such information is basic to the planning and development of human and health care services.

There is information about the Hispanic elderly's economic condition to include poverty levels, sources of income, amount of Social Security pensions, and numbers receiving SSI, all indicators of need and vulnerability. But, relatively little is known about "cultural" factors that influence life styles and world views that guide behaviors; less is known about the role of language as a reflector of culture and its uses in a variety of cognitive processes. We also know little about Hispanic group cultural and linguistic differences determined by country of origin, date of immigration to the United States, degree of acculturation and urbanization, ethnicity and/or race. Until there are on-going efforts over time to explore fully not only the nature of the variables that determine culture and language needs but their role in defining quality of life and well-being for these groups of elderly, efforts to improve the access and use of human services by the various populations of Hispanic elderly will remain speculative.

Caregiving and the Intergenerational Family

As a person ages, the composition of his or her family and the roles of family members change. For example, the elderly have numerous family roles as spouses, parents, grandparents, relatives of other kinds, and sometimes children of very old parents. Moreover, these changing sets of family relationships are often accompanied by changes in adjusting to life situations associated with aging, illness or death of a spouse, one's own illness, physical impairments, retirement, reduced income, presence of grandchildren, and expanded support networks which may include social service and health care agencies (Zopf, 1986). In times of need, the elderly may have to turn to those who once depended on them for financial and emotional support and health care. In cases where adult children are not available, other relatives, neighbors, and outside agencies expand the social support network of the elderly. The elderly also reciprocate by providing instrumental and emotional support as needed by their children and other relatives and friends.

The presence of intergenerational networks of support is well-documented in the research literature. However, little information is available on how different cultural groups respond to or use intergenerational networks. Assistance during time of need (e.g., during illness) is a significant indicator of the nature and availability of intergenerational support. In many industrialized societies the family has traditionally had the major responsibility for taking care of the sick elderly. However, there has been a tremendous increase in the number of nursing homes, hospitals, and home health care agencies that now provide such care. Traditional family functions related to instrumental and emotional support are also being replaced by agencies specializing in providing home health aides, homemakers, transportation aids, and social workers. Some governmental agencies also go so far as to provide income support for the elderly.

Yet, despite alternative help sources, family help continues to play an important role in support of the elderly (Shanas, 1986). Intergenerational support is especially important among those families who are in the greatest social and economic need, the major reason being that "access to services remains a major problem for elderly citizens who are poor, disabled, frail, living in rural areas, members of ethnic minority groups and uninsured" (Kauffman, Randolph, Drake & Gelfand, 1987, p.4).

For Hispanic families, institutional settings such as nursing homes and hospitals are not attractive options . Lower levels of income during their working years and consequent lower levels of Social Security benefits and pensions render them unable to afford such services. Instrumental and emotional support provided by other specialized agencies is not affordable and may not be culturally specific. Problems with applying traditional helping techniques to a culturally different population and language barriers are often cited as major reasons why these specialized services are unattractive to the Hispanic elderly and their families. Thus, for Hispanic families, the elderly may have to depend on mutual assistance and reciprocal

support among their social network to a larger extent than is usually
found in contemporary society.

There is a substantial body of literature documenting
extensive intergenerational support networks and their social
significance (Adams, 1968; Hays & Mindel, 1973; Israel & Antonucci,
1987; Mutran, 1986; Shanas, 1967, 1986; Sussman, 1959; Troll,
1971). Family help in time of illness, exchange of services, and
visiting are common among the elderly and their children and
relatives whether or not they live in the same household (Shanas,
1986). Based on data from Blacks & Whites in the 1975 national
survey of the non-institutionalized community aged, Shanas (1986)
concluded that:

1. the immediate family of the elderly is the major social
   support of the elderly in time of illness; and
2. the extended family of the elderly (through personal
   visits) is the major tie of the elderly to the community.

She further notes that "such patterns are indicators of the mutual
expectations of each generation for the other" (p.96). Support for
cultural interpretations is provided by Mutran's (1986) examination of
intergenerational support among Blacks and Whites. Most notably
among the observed differences was the influence of attitudes,
primarily that of respect, on helping behavior. This was supported
by Wylie's (1970) conclusion that Blacks are more likely than Whites
to regard the elderly with respect. A growing body of research
suggests a positive relationship between social networks, social
support, physical, and mental health (Israel & Antonucci, 1987).

In general, families experience a significant amount of
reciprocal help between older and younger relatives that may

continue throughout the life span of that family. It is assumed that expectations to receive help from family members grow with age and that the use of formal human services will increase as the family and other informal sources of support decrease. For example, there is sufficient evidence to the effect that hospitalization or institutional placements most frequently occur either because the patient lacks a natural support system or because existing supports have broken down due to changes in the life of other family members (Lowenthal, 1964).

In addition to the increased reliance on family for most caregiving responsibilities as one ages, there are other social and demographic trends that will increase expectations from primary caregivers and that should have profound implications in the planning and delivery of services. The replacement of chronic illnesses for acute diseases that account for most deaths early in this century is an example. People are living longer today even after the onset of chronic disease and disability. Thus, it is accurate to assume that fewer people will reach the end of life without experiencing some period of dependency. More years of dependency mean more years during which there must be someone on whom to depend. As such, long term care has become a normative experience, expectable though usually unplanned (Brody, 1985). Furthermore, it is predominantly women who provide such care and share their homes when the elderly cannot manage their own needs. This leads to the concern for the role strain being put on "women in the middle," or middle-aged women who are torn between conflicting demands of the work place, their own families, and the responsibilities to care for older relatives as well as their own children.

Depression, anxiety, frustration, and emotional exhaustion
are frequently reported by caregivers who find themselves with
restrictions of time and freedom, isolation, and conflict from
competing demand of their various roles and responsibilities. It is no
surprise that women who comprise the bulk of caregivers point to the
difficulties found in setting their own personal priorities and life style
"interference" that inevitably affect the family's activities (Cantor,
1983). It is not surprising that most caregivers perceive their relatives
as lonely and/or depressed, but seem to feel unable to be both
friend and counselor as well as responsible family members
(Horowitz, 1982).

The growing realization and acknowledgement that some
form of family support exists for most older people raises questions
regarding the consequences to the family unit inherent in providing
care to older relatives on a long-term basis. The renewed public
acceptance of the social-care functions performed by the family, and
their success in coping with the stresses resulting from caring for
their aging relatives, are clearly relevant to the understanding of the
elderly person's feelings of well-being. Stresses, real or potential,
are multiple and burdensome. Thus, it has been suggested that no
family caregiver is immune from perpetrating abuse given the stress
of the caregiving task and the caregiver's lack of skills required to
carry out such tasks (Kosberg, 1980). As indicated above, the
emotional consequences of caregiving have been found to be
numerous, with feelings of depression, low morale, and emotional
exhaustion being the most stressful to family caregivers. It is no
surprise that children want to maintain a central role in relation to their
parents, but not to be the only source of help (Cicerelly, 1981).

The Hispanic Family and Caregiving Functions

In contrast to the research that is available on caregiving among the general population of elderly, research on any aspect of the Hispanic elderly is either lacking or at early descriptive phases. Zúñiga-Martínez' (1979) doctoral dissertation deals with the inter-generational attitudes of 193 Mexican-Americans in the city of San Diego, California. The population itself, according to her findings, presents a different social stratification pattern than that of the majority population and thus seems to refer to a different set of problems for the aged. Streib (1978) mentions several features which are distinct to the Hispanic population among which two are relevant to this paper. These are higher dependency ratios and an emphasis on the modified extended family defined as layers of blood-related and non-related relatives and members of other informal networks, e.g. *compadres* and *comadres* and not neces-sarily living in the same household. Past research (Kluckhohn & Strodtbeck, 1961; Clark, 1959; Rubel, 1966) and more recent research (Sotomayor, 1973; Bastida, 1979) point out that Mexican-American and Puerto Ricans are more closely involved with a local kin group than are others in the majority society and support the idea that the extended family is a vital social support system that includes a special role for the elderly family members.

Thus, the presence of this closely-knit extended family has been presented as an advantage for Hispanics. Mutual family support has been viewed as an aid in managing not only the general stresses of daily living, but also the stresses related to being a member of an ethnic minority group.

Montiel (1978), in his analysis of the Hispanic family, concluded that while there are substantial differences in the make-up of
the Hispanic family among and within the various Hispanic sub-
groups, there are some values and cultural attributes generally
shared by most Hispanics. Help-giving/help-receiving interactions
between the Hispanic elderly and their families were found to be
common characteristics. According to Sotomayor (1973), Sánchez-
Mayers (1985), and Maldonado (1985), the reciprocal supportive
relationship that exists between older Hispanics and their families
serves as a source of mutual support and/or protection, especially
during times of crisis. Valle & Martínez (1981), Valle & Mendoza
(1978), Mayers (1980), Keef, Padilla, & Carlos (1978), Becerra &
Shaw (1984) have also analyzed the reciprocal supportive relationship which exists between Hispanic elderly and their families. They
note that the help-giving/help-receiving interaction is essential to the
well-being of all the family members.

Another view is argued by Croach (1972) who suggests that
the extended Mexican-American family may be a myth and that the
elderly have no expectations that their children will take care of them
as they age or become dependent. Maldonado (1975) raises
questions about the irreversible effects of modernization and
growing family mobility on family values that can change the role
and status of the Hispanic elderly within their own family units.
Laurel (1976) found younger generation Mexican-Americans
departing from traditional views of roles in relation to caring for aged
parents. Markides, Martin, & Gómez (1983) in an ethnic comparative
study in Texas found little indication that older Mexican-Americans
are in a more advantageous position than older Anglos as far as

being cared for by their own family networks. The argument continues whether the recent deterioration of the traditional Hispanic family, the degree of interdependence and mutual assistance has significantly eroded. But, little empirical evidence exists to substantiate the assumption that the longstanding supportive and reciprocal relationship which has existed between Hispanic elderly and their families has indeed changed.

Despite the dearth of research specifically on the topic of caregiving within the Hispanic family, there is no reason to question that both parents and children experience psychological stress as both parties attempt to meet cultural prescriptions that the elderly must be cared for within the family. When an elderly parent is no longer able to care for himself/herself and moves into the household of a married son or daughter, many problems inevitably will arise that can disrupt the living condition of that family. The children in an Hispanic home, like in any other non-Hispanic family, can resent the loss of privacy that occurs when someone moves into their home; ways of coping with dissent and conflict assume a different style and the entire family must modify their behaviors to accommodate the elderly family members. How the various Hispanic family members, including the elderly, adjust and cope with such changes is an important question. The authors recognize that Hispanics in the United States are a heterogeneous population. For purposes of this study and in view of the limited data, Puerto Ricans and Mexican-Americans are seen as sharing similar family values as they pertain to reciprocal help-giving patterns, factors that determine a sense of well-being, and mastery in relation to self-esteem.

The Purpose of this Study

In an effort to identify components that should guide the development of bicultural and bilingual human services for Hispanic elderly, this study sought to examine variables that are perceived as integral elements of culture within the broader context of basic emotional needs, specifically well-being and a sense of mastery. Reciprocal helping patterns provided by family members of the Hispanic elderly, the effect of help giving and help receiving on the self-esteem and sense of mastery of the elderly, and perceived health status as a determinant of self-esteem and mastery, were selected for analysis.

As the number of Hispanic elderly will grow, the need for caregiving will also increase. Thus the findings of this study will provide important preliminary guidelines to future research in all aspects of the caregiving tasks and the subsequent development of services for the Hispanic elderly.

Despite this growing body of research on social support and its importance to the elderly's psychological and physical well-being, little or no attention has been given to help patterns among Hispanic families, who represent the fastest growing segment of the U. S. population . This paper presents preliminary data on the instrumental and emotional supports provided to the Hispanic elderly by family members and others. Specifically, the analyses focused on generating descriptive statistics for receipt of support, provision of support, and family contact.

Preliminary data on mutual assistance and reciprocal support patterns are also presented. Although specific relationships between support patterns and well-being are not investigated, the descriptive information on the nature of helping patterns among Hispanic families is expected to provide useful directions for future research and policy.

Method

The data presented in this paper come from a larger study on Hispanic elderly and was collected from a sample of low-income Hispanic respondents 65 years old or older. The sample design used four sites that produced a multi-state area sample. Two primarily urban areas located in different parts of the country were selected: Hartford, Connecticut and San Antonio, Texas. Two primarily rural sites were selected: the Rio Grande Valley of South Texas and Northern New Mexico. Criteria for inclusion in the study included five years or more residence in the U.S., lack of an incapacitating physical ailment and willingness to participate in the study.

Sampling units in the urban areas were primary sampling units (PSU) of the U.S. Bureau of the Census. Enumeration districts were used as the primary sampling units for the rural areas. The enumeration districts were randomly selected and within that enumeration district only one area was selected for inclusion. One-half of the respondents were selected as a "community sample" and the other half were households known to social service agencies. These clients were listed and then random selection was made from that list.

Three-hundred and forty-seven interviews were conducted. The study instrument contained questions on:
1. help received from family,
2. help given to family,

3. family involvement in specific important life events,

4. level of satisfaction with help received from family, and

5. respect received from family.

Sample Characteristics

Of the total sample of 347 respondents, 238 (69%) were females and 109 (31%) were males. The ages ranged from 62 to 97 years, with a median age of 73 years. Over two-thirds (67%) of the respondents lived alone. Eighty seven (25%) lived with others, and only a few (8%) lived with a spouse. More than half of both males and females (54%) and (60%) respectively were born outside the United States. Thus, the sample population was primarily an immigrant one.

Measures

A 9-item scale was used to measure help received from family and other sources with activities such as transportation, minor household repairs, housekeeping, and automobile care. Respondents were asked whether or not they received help with any of the areas included in the scale and who had provided such help. For help given to family, a 10-item scale was used. Items in this scale asked questions about baby-sitting with grandchildren, financial help to children, looking after a son or daughter when ill and helping children with important decisions. The elderly respondent's satisfaction with family level of support and respect was measured through a series of open-ended questions which addressed level of help, love and respect received from their children and other relatives.

Results
Help Received From Family

Table 1
Reports of Help Received by Hispanic Elderly from Social Support Systems. (Frequency and Percentage)

Type of Help/Service (N=347)	Help Received	
	F	%
Transportation	256	(74)
Care when Ill	228	(66)
Shopping	215	(62)
Making Important Decisions	208	(59)
Paying Taxes, Bills, etc.	192	(55)
Housekeeping/Washing	190	(55)
Minor Repairs	184	(53)
Legal Aid	155	(45)
Car Care	73	(21)

As shown in Table 1, the Hispanic elderly in this study received a wide range of help/services from their social support systems. Nearly three-fourths reported that they received help with transportation (74%). Other frequently reported types of help/service included: help when ill (66%), shopping (62%) and making important decisions (59%). Over half of the respondents also reported that they received help with paying taxes and bills (55%),

Table 2

Table 2

Respondents Reports of Who Provides Help to them by Type of Help (Percentages)

N=347

Type of Help /Service	Social Service Agency	Son	Daughter	Grandchild	Other Relatives In-Laws	Nephews	Neighbors	Spouse	Self	Missing
Transportation	15	11	17	3	4	5	5	4	22	15
Care When Ill	2	13	28	1	4	4	4	4	25	16
Shopping	3	10	18	2	4	3	3	5	34	18
Make Important Decisions	2	14	19	1	3	3	1	6	29	21
Paying Taxes, Bills, etc.	2	8	14	1	3	4	1	7	35	24
Housekeeping/Washing	5	3	12	1	3	4	2	4	45	22
Minor Repairs	13	19	4	1	4	2	3	4	21	30
Legal Aid	8	11	12	1	1	1	2	1	19	42
Car Care	1	8	4	0	1	0	1	3	16	67

Table 3

Respondents Reports of Type of Help Given to Family by How often Given (Percentages)

Table 3

Type of Help Given	Always	Sometimes	Rarely	Never	Does not apply	Missing
How often is help Given ? (%)						
Babysit Grandchildren	6	14	13	40	10	16
Providing Financial Help to Children	5	9	19	44	10	14
Providing Counseling When Children Have Problems	30	9	9	14	8	14
Take Grandchildren Into Home When Problem Exists at Home	7	9	8	41	17	18
Looked After Children When Ill	15	13	11	32	15	14
Took In Unemployed Son or Daughter	13	11	7	39	14	16
Help Children With Important Decisions	21	21	13	25	8	13
Take Son/Daughter Out of Jail	2	2	5	50	21	21
Provide Religious Instruction To Grandchildren	19	16	8	28	8	21

housekeeping/washing (55%), and minor household repairs (53%). Respondents were least likely to report that they received legal aid (45%) or help with automobile care (21%).

Table 2 shows that the Hispanic elderly tend to rely on themselves more than anyone else in getting services they need or want. However, when help is provided by others, it appears that, for all but three services, daughters were the most frequently reported helper. For two of the other services (minor house repairs and auto care), sons were the most frequently reported helpers. For the third service (legal aid), daughters and sons are reported by similar percentages (12% and 11%, respectively). Social service agencies appear to be a frequent source of help only for transportation (15%) and legal aid (8%).

Additional helpers appear to come from the "other relatives" group (grandchildren, in-laws, nephews), and are reported more frequently than "spouses" for all services except auto care. It also appears from Table 2 that "neighbors" are reported with the same frequency as "spouses" for transportation, minor house repairs, shopping, care when ill, and legal assistance.

Table 3 indicates that the Hispanic elderly always or sometimes provide help to their families in the form of counseling children when they have problems (39%), helping children with important decisions (42%), providing religious instruction to grandchildren (35%), and looking after their children when ill (28%). Less than a quarter reported that they took in an unemployed son or daughter (24%), provided baby-sitting for their grandchildren (20%), took grandchildren into their homes when there were problems (16%), or provided financial help to their children (13%). Very few

(4%) reported that they had taken a son or daughter out of jail. (Note: most (42%) of the responses to this latter item were coded as "does not apply" or "missing").

Data in Table 4 indicate that most Hispanic elderly inter-viewed were satisfied with the amount of help they received from their families. Many of them agreed that they were both respected (73%) and loved by their children (70%). Most reported that their children's love was demonstrated by visiting them (46%) and checking on their needs (16%). Grandchildren's love was demonstrated by visiting them (28%) and spending time with them (10%). They also reported that help would be available to them from their families if needed (72%). On the other hand, the data in Table 4, indicate that 42 percent of the total sample interviewed reported not being satisfied with the level of personal contact that they had with relatives and *compadres/comadres*.

The majority of those interviewed who indicated expe-riencing significant life events within the past five years (e.g. physical illness, death in family, legal problems, substance abuse and/or mental illness within family, etc.), reported that emotional support and counseling were the type of support most often available and that daughters, followed by sons, were the most involved in providing such help. One such case which illustrates family involvement during stressful situations is that of Mr. Garza, a 78-year-old widowed male with four years of formal education. About a month before he was interviewed, Mr. Garza's 45-year-old son had died of a brain tumor. In the interview Mr. Garza stated:

> *I would not know what to do if my other sons and daughters had not rallied around me. The support my children*

Table 4

Level of Satisfaction that Hispanic Elderly have toward their family as measured by the amount of respect and love they feel they receive from their families, how often they see relatives, and whether or not relatives are available to help them (Frequency and Percent)

	F	%
HAVE CHILDREN SHOWN LOVE?		
Strongly agree	177	51
Agree	66	19
Not sure	15	4
Disagree	12	4
Strongly disagree	15	4
Missing	62	18
HOW HAVE CHILDREN DEMONSTRATED LOVE?		
Do not visit	29	8
Visit often	159	46
Check on your needs	55	16
Remember family events	6	2
Offers financial help	26	1
Does not apply	13	4
Other	10	3
Missing	66	19
HOW HAVE GRANDCHILDRED DEMONSTRATED LOVE?		
Do not visit	29	8
Visit often	96	28
Check on your needs	13	4
Spend time	34	10
Provide services and help	7	2
None	10	3
Missing	158	46
DO YOU BELIEVE YOUR CHILDREN RESPECT YOU?		
Yes	253	73
No	14	4
Missing	80	23
SEE RELATIVE AS MUCH AS WANT		
Dissatisfied	72	21
Not too often	76	22
Frequently	172	50
Missing	27	8

	F	%
ARE RELATIVES AVAILABLE FOR HELP WHEN IN NEED?		
No	38	11
From time to time	40	12
For short time	47	14
All the time	163	47
Missing	59	17

> *provided was important in getting me through the first few weeks after this event. I still feel every sad and lonely, but having my children around me makes me feel a little better*

Another illustration on the importance that family involvement plays in coping with stressful life events is the case of Mrs. Martínez. She is a 68-year-old woman with 11 years of formal education and an annual income of $8,000. Mrs. Martínez considers herself to be in fair health. The significant event mentioned during her interview was the death of her husband:

> *My husband's death affected my health for about three years. I was very depressed. But, my daughter's daily visits kept me going. She always told me how important it was for me to keep my spirits up, not to give up. I am glad that I have her near me.*

Discussion

These preliminary findings clearly indicate that the Hispanic elderly are involved in reciprocal relationships with their families for instrumental support when ill, making important decisions, and handling financial problems. These findings are similar to those reported by Shanas (1986): the immediate family is the major source of support to the elderly in time of illness. Furthermore, the elderly appear more likely to receive help than to be depended on to give help in these situations. Two-thirds received help when they were ill (40% received help from children); but just slightly more than a quarter provided help to ill children. Three-fifths received help with making important decisions (33% from children); while two-fifths provided such help to children. Finally, over half received help with financial matters (23% from children), while less than 15% provided financial help to their children. As indicated, most of these reciprocal relationships involved the elderly's adult children, primarily daughters and to a lesser extent sons. This finding is also similar to reports in previous research.

There is an imbalance in the exchanges (Shanas,1979; Troll,1971) of service reported above that may be due to the need for help and the ability to provide assistance. With respect to illness and financial problems, the elderly may have had a greater need for help than their adult children due to the nature of their illness and reduced income. For these same reasons, the elderly may have been less able to provide care for ill children (or provide financial support); or the children may have required less assistance because their illness was not serious or they had adequate income or alternative helpers. On the other hand, in making important decisions, the elderly were more likely to provide help (42%) than to receive help (33%), suggesting that their children consulted them on matters with which they needed assistance and with which the elderly had some ability to assist. The data for other instrumental tasks such as assisting with transportation, shopping, and household repairs did not allow for an examination of reciprocal relationships. However, the data indicate that the Hispanic elderly also depend primarily on their adult children for assistance with these activities. In "exchange" the elderly provide instrumental support for their children in a variety of ways, including: taking unemployed children into their home, bailing adult children out of jail, baby-sitting for grandchildren, taking grandchildren into their home when a problem exists at the adult child's home, and providing religious instruction to grand-children. In addition, 40% of the elderly reported that they provide counseling when their children have problems. These findings support the notion that family functions change as one ages and must make adjustments (Zopf, 1986).

These data also suggest that both the need for help and the variety in support provided may reflect the special socioeconomic circumstances of the Hispanic elderly and their families.The Hispanic elderly in this study were in the lower socioeconomic group and, thus, may have had more acute needs for help. Their children were also likely to be in this group and, thus, also may have had acute needs for help. Consequently, the ability to furnish assistance may have been dictated by these socioeconomic realities. Future research should seek to clarify the influence of socioeconomic factors on helping patterns. Caution should be exercised so as not to be misled by the assumption of homogeneity among Hispanic populations.

A significant unknown that cannot be addressed by these preliminary data is the extent to which these reciprocal relationships arc beneficial or detrimental to the physical and psychological well-being of the Hispanic elderly. For example, over a third reported that they provided religious instruction to grandchildren. Through this one activity, the Hispanic elderly can fulfill two needs. In addition to performing an important family function (even if they are physically limited), the elderly are also able to make meaningful use of their leisure time. This suggests that religious instruction may be an appropriate use of leisure time for Hispanic elderly and outside agencies should consider this in developing programs for them. On the other hand, the Hispanic elderly's frequent involvement in stressful life events of their adult children (assisting with financial problems, child care when there is a problem in the child's home, bailing out of jail, and counseling for personal problems) suggests that these family roles may adversely affect the Hispanic elderly who are themselves at risk for experiencing a long list of problems. A practical response to this situation might be a program of comprehensive family services where adult children can refer or get assistance with problems of the elderly and, conversely, the elderly can refer or get assistance with problems of their adult children. From an empirical standpoint, additional research is needed to understand the extent to which participation in a reciprocal and/or intergenerational support relationship benefits or disadvantages the Hispanic elderly.

Previous research suggests that instrumental support and reciprocal instrumental support are not significantly related to psychological well-being (Israel & Antonnuci, 1987). However, in the earlier study instrumental support was limited to care when ill. Future research should, therefore, further seek to clarify the extent to which benefits of reciprocity may differ by the type of support provided. Research is also needed to determine whether or not the Hispanic elderly and their families perceive support from formal helping sources as attractive options. Such research should also incorporate attitudinal factors with patterns of helping behavior to clarify the Hispanic elderly's perceptions of formal agency support (that is, would they use formal agencies and, if so, under what circumstance?).

Other factors that should receive emphasis in future research include: satisfaction with support, exchange of services with helpers other than adult children, cultural and linguistic factors that influence patterns of helping behavior, and size, density and frequency of interaction with helpers. Since previous research consistently indicates that emotional support and reciprocal emotional support are significantly related to psychological well-being (Israel & Antonucci, 1987), emphasis in future research should also be placed on examining additional areas of emotional support. The effects of reciprocal emotional support on physical health status should also be investigated. Poverty, inadequate health-care benefits, limited access to health and social services, minority group status, isolation from native culture, and other cultural and linguistic barriers prevent a substantial portion of the Hispanic population from experiencing an optimal quality of life. The additional problems associated with aging complicate this situation for the Hispanic elderly. The data presented in this paper suggest that some of their problems can be addressed through existing social support net-works (reciprocal support relationships with their families). However, the extent to which these networks can adequately address these problems is unknown. Formal helping sources should seek to incorporate these informal helping networks into their programming for the Hispanic elderly until other interventions are evaluated or further research is conducted to clarify some of the empirical issues outlined in this paper.

These preliminary data, when considered with previous work in this area, suggest that there are benefits in the mutuality relationship that can be improved upon to ensure an optimal quality of life.

PART II:

Theoretical and Methodological Implications of the Cultural Context of Coping

Reexamining Assumptions About Extended Familism: Older Puerto Ricans in a Comparative Perspective

Elena Bastida, Ph.D.

Repeatedly, assumptions have been made in the gerontological literature in reference to the possible effect that various aspects of the modernization process may have had and have on the status of the Hispanic elderly. Modernization theory, as Hendricks & Hendricks note (1986) had become a central feature of the vocabulary of international social science by the time aging research was beginning to fashion its own theories. Based on the premises of this theory, or rather the various ideas and perspectives that became known as modernization theory, a conceptual framework was laid for cross cultural and historical comparisons of the status of the elderly. With each successive phase of development, all aspects of a society were thought to move away from diffused activities based on closed, ascriptive status systems with extended kinship networks to technologically intensive, industrial economies based on achieved status. By means of secondary carriers of modernization, language, religion, and other beliefs systems, new cultural values appear to justify the emergent dimension of the human experience. At each stage these values increasingly stress secular, instrumental rationality and contractual relationships. Since instrumental or economic rationality becomes the defining criterion for all events, inevitably, similar arrangements will evolve and revise the bases of personal identity (Eisenstadt, 1974). With rapid social change, Simmons (1960) observes, the structural framework that favored the elderly, ensured their power, and buttressed their seniority rights disappeared as their roles are taken and allocated to the young.

In discussing the aging experience of older Hispanics, gerontologists have made allusions to the premises of modernization theory in questioning how the changes that have taken place in modern industrial society have affected the status and life experience of older Hispanics in the United States. For example, Maldonado (1975) cautions against the assumption made by the early literature on Hispanics which frequently contended that intergenerational help and assistance, particularly among Mexican-Americans, was customary. Maldonado observes:

> Social scientists both within the Mexican-American community and without, have created sociological and psychological theories that supposedly explain and describe the elderly Chicanos. This was especially true of the concepts of the extended family and of the patriarchal or matriarchal structure, which refers in this instance to the high status and the roles of the family's older members. However, it is becoming questionable whether these theories now describe this particular segment of the Chicano community.

Similarly, it has been said of the disadvantages facing the Puerto Rican elderly when traditional values are likely to fade and the second generation takes on the cultural values of Anglo society. Schaefer (1984) notes: "the less important role played by the extended family is unfortunate,... As familism declines and the extended family weakens, Puerto Ricans will be forced to turn to impersonal bureaucratic agencies for the type of services that used to be provided by the kinfolk." Maldonado finds that notions about traditional familism and the extended family work to the disadvantage of aged Mexican-Americans rather than have positive consequences for their well-being. He notes that Mexican-Americans may be routinely excluded from aging programs that could greatly enhance their quality of life since it is wrongly assumed that the extended family is meeting all of their needs.

More recent findings have shown that there are, in fact, significant members of the Hispanic-American elderly living alone (U.S. Census, 1985; Lacayo, et al., 1980). Hendricks & Hendricks (1986) propose that, whether the process of acculturation gradually erodes the traditional role of the Hispanic American aged or whether they continue to live their lives free of the discontinuities some feel characteristic of the Anglo aged is debatable; however, at least among the present generation, there is still a place for the elderly .

Socio-Structural Characteristics

In discussing the socio-cultural framework that gives meaning to the aging experience of older Hispanics, it becomes important to examine how their aging experience may vary with the structural characteristics of the community of residence. Put simply, there is a phenomenon of community context that has consequences, or so we have assumed, for the elderly.

At present, variants of the socio-environmental perspective are being developed by gerontologists to explain both individual or structural levels of personal well-being (Hendricks & Hendrichs, 1986). Since the mid 1970's, theory in social gerontology has begun to consider structural variations and the nature or the distinctive qualities of the social relations growing out of the organization of different social systems as an important analytical concern. In this chapter we explore some of these new theoretical formulations by examining differences in the aging experience of older sup-populations of Hispanics residing in structurally different communities where variations are found in the density of the ethnic concentration, urban-rural populations, economic differentiation and regional location.

Purpose and Scope of the Chapter

The focus of this chapter lies in empirically testing some of the already noted assumptions of modernization theory by presenting and discussing data gathered from two subpopulations of older Hispanics, Mexican-Americans and Puerto Ricans, at four regionally different sites. In realizing this purpose, the chapter has been divided into three parts. Part I introduces the overall methodology of the study and includes a brief description of the sites and sampling procedures. Part II presents a detailed profile of older Puerto Ricans in Hartford, Connecticut. This profile is necessary since nowhere else in this book an in-depth examination of older Puerto Ricans is presented. Finally, Part III compares and contrasts salient characteristics of this population with those of older Mexican Americans residing in three geographically and structurally different sites. No detailed account of these sub populations has been found necessary since other chapters in the book extensively deal with them.

PART I
Methodology

Four different communities were selected for study. These communities were Hartford, CT., San Antonio, TX., Northern rural New Mexico, and McAllen, TX. The criteria used for the selection of these cities were:

1. high Hispanic population concentration;
2. Puerto Rican and Mexican origin populations;
3. high concentration of family units; and
4. potential concentration of Hispanic persons 65 years of age and over.

The unit of study was households. In instances where the household consisted of an elderly couple, both were interviewed. However, the forty-four conjoint interviews that were made were not included in the analysis presented here due to methodological difficulties in assessing the appropriate respondent.

The sampling plan developed at each of the four sites took into account the unique characteristics of each geographical location with the objective of producing a multi-stage area sample. Primary sampling units for Standard Metropolitan Areas of the Bureau of the Census were used to identify the samples in the two large metropolitan areas, Hartford, Connecticut and San Antonio, Texas. Enumeration districts were used in the identification of the sample in the primarily rural site of Northern New Mexico and in the smaller urban area of McAllen, Texas. Enumeration districts were particularly helpful in obtaining detailed information on the location and size of the isolated, hard-to-reach rural hamlets in New Mexico.

Selection of elderly subjects was limited to those elderly

Hispanics who had resided in the United States for a minimum of ten years, who were not affected by an incapacitating physical ailment, and who were willing to participate in the study as volunteers. Due to the recent growth of the Puerto Rican population in Hartford, and their recent migration to that city, it was decided to use five years of local residence rather than ten years.

Combined sampling procedures were used to identify the sample. These techniques included the more rigorous area pro-bability sampling procedure discussed above and purposive sampling techniques. Purposive sampling was obtained through a careful screening of participants from agencies providing services to the targeted population from which lists were drawn containing participants' names. Two samples were obtained based on the two sampling procedures, one based on area probability sampling, the other on purposive techniques.

Given our emphasis on Puerto Ricans in this chapter, we will give a short description of the sampling procedure employed in obtaining the Hartford sample. Due to the recent immigration of Puerto Ricans to the city of Hartford, the actual population size is not accurately reflected in the 1980 Bureau Census data. Thus, the Hartford Primary Census Units listed in the 1980 Census were used to identify the census tracks with (1) large numbers of Hispanics and (2) large numbers of individuals 65 years of age and over. Four census tracks known to have large Hispanic populations were canvassed and placed in a sampling frame. Moreover, the Hartford Housing Authority was contacted to obtain a list of Puerto Rican elderly living in public housing located outside of the above mentioned census tracks who otherwise might be overlooked due to their characteristically high mobility rates. By combining the census track population with the public housing population, a list of 400 elderly Puerto Ricans was compiled which included over half of the Puerto Rican elderly population in the Hartford Standard Metropolitan Area. From this list, seventy-five (75) individuals were selected at random and contacted personally to determine interest in participating in the study. Fifty agreed to participate. Another fifty respondents were obtained through the efforts of the Institute for the Hispanic Family, a local counseling agency. All Puerto Rican elderly who had requested services in the five year period preceding the study were identified and placed in a list of 400 persons from which the study sample was randomly selected. A total sample of 95 persons was identified for the Hartford area.

Interviews lasted approximately two hours and for the Puerto Rican sample were always conducted in Spanish, since this was their language of preference. All interviews were conducted at the respondents' homes.

The Concept of Social Support System

In urban industrial society, the support system of the elderly increasingly involves an amalgam of informal services provided by family, friends, and neighbors and formal services provided by the private and public sections. Within this type of social structure, as Litwak (1965) has noted, kinship structures have gradually evolved from the traditional extended family to the modified extended family in which a coalition of separately housed, semi-autonomous nuclear families operates in a state of partial dependency with shared family functions. Thus it could only be expected that along with this evolution in family structure there would be an accompanying shift in the role of family and society with respect to the elderly. Thus, as Cantor (1979) notes, today the United States government provides the floor of basic services for older people in such crucial areas as income maintenance, housing, health, safety, and transportation. But family and significant others retain considerable importance in meeting the more idiosyncratic social support needs of the individual.

A social support system can be broadly defined as encompassing those informal and formal activities as well as personal support services required by the elderly in order to remain independently in the community (Cantor, 1979). Such a support system includes both the formal and informal components. In addition to enabling the older person to carry out the tasks of daily living, support systems provide for opportunities for socialization and personal assistance during times of illness or crisis. Informal network members are selected by the elderly principally from among kin, friends and neighbors.

Three levels of the informal personal support system of older people have been identified in the literature (Cantor, 1979). These are kin, close friends, and neighbors, each with a complementary role to play. These three levels comprise six separate elements: four are part of the kinship structure--spouse, child, sibling, and other relatives; and two, friends and neighbors, involve unrelated individuals usually living in geographical proximity to the elderly. For the purposes of our data analysis and discussion, the emphasis here is on the family, particularly children, and on the extent and type of relationship that occurs between older people and their kin.

In this chapter we examine the relationship of ethnicity, in this case Hispanic origin, to the prevalence of the extended family and the extent to which this structure provides an informal support system of helping relationships. Other possible indicators of traditionality, e.g. religious beliefs, church attendance, strong cultural preferences, are also investigated as we reexamine the "traditional" assumptions made in reference to the Hispanic elderly.

PART II
The Puerto Rican Sample

A total of 85 Puerto Ricans were interviewed. Of these, 30 were males and 55 were females. For this subpopulation, Spanish was unanimously their languare of preference. The median age for males was 65-69; only 3 males were over 80 years of age. The median age for females was also 65-69 with 4 women reporting 80 years of age and older. The Puerto Rican sample had the fewest octogenarians among all the subpopulations studied. A total of 7 Puerto Ricans were 80 years of age and older in contrast to a total of 27, 19 and 20 for the San Antonio, New Mexico and South Texas samples respectively.

Only 8 Puerto Ricans were married; 43 were widowed; 27 were divorced or separated; and 4 were single. Similarly to the other subpopulations, older Puerto Ricans had few, if any, years of formal school completed. Only 2 men were high school graduates and none of the women had completed high school. In fact, only 8 women had completed between 5 and 8 years of school.

Of the 85 Puerto Ricans, only one reported part-time work with 84 indicating that they were retired. Of the men, 10 were retired on disability. Their employment status reflected their lack of education and a lifetime of low socioeconomic status.

Of the 28 men who reported their lifetime employment status, 13 were farm laborers, 9 were craftsmen. 5 were service workers and 1 was an operative. Similarly, the women had held employment in low-paying jobs which usually carried no fringe benefits or any type of security. Thirty-three women reported work in private households, 16 were farm laborers, 4 had worked in the service industry, 2 were operatives and one had been a craftswoman.

Informal Support System of Older Puerto Ricans

A series of criterion variables was selected to describe the extent and operation of the informal support sytem. Examples of such measures include the likelihood of living with a spouse, total number of relatives who lived in the proximity, total number of children, total number of children who were functional, frequency of seeing children, frequency of seeing relatives, amount of help child gives parents, types of help child gives parents and by parents to children. Although these separate variables could perhaps have been combined into single measures of the extent of the informal support system and the degree of interaction between the elderly and the various support components, a fuller picture is derived by discussing the most salient aspects of the informal support system separately.

Nine types of assistance from child-to-parent and 10 types from parent-to-child were listed. Based on the different types of assistance and following Cantor (1979), four broad categories of help were established.

1. crisis interaction - help during illness or any other major family crisis

2. assistance with chores of daily living - baby-sitting, shopping, transportation, keeping house, fixing things in the house, car maintenance

3. advice giving - child rearing, home management, money matters

4. gift giving - monetary assistance and non monetary presents

Before going into the details of the types of assistance provided, it is important to note that 15 of the Puerto Rican men and 48 of the women reported that someone helped them whenever necessary. When asked who was their major helper, 13 gave their sons as their major helper, while 31 indicated their daughters. No Puerto Rican elderly indicated a formal provider to be a major source of assistance.

Forty one elderly Puerto Ricans had a person who checked on them daily, while 43 had a once-a-day call from someone who could help if necessary. Of those who reported to have a person who checked on them daily, 29 listed their daughters, 8 listed their sons and 4 listed a neighbor.

The type of assistance most frequently given to the elderly was transportation. Eighteen of the elderly received assistance from their daughters, while 12 received assistance from their sons. Of significance, however, is the fact that this is the one type of assistance where either a formal agency or other relative appears to provide as much assistance to the elderly. For example, 23 respondents indicated other relatives while 15 indicated a formal agency. Only 7 respondents indicated that they provided their own transportation. Still, children provided the most assistance when combining the daughter and son categories.

Two other types of assistance were frequently given to the respondents by their children, these were assistance with shopping and housekeeping. Again, in these two categories daughters were given as the most frequent type of helper. Forty-one respondents indicated that their daughters took them shopping, while 14 said their sons provided this assistance. Only daughters were listed as providing daily assistance with housekeeping (n=31). Twenty-six respondents indicated that their children had helped them on a daily basis while they were ill and 32 said they could count on this type of assistance whenever it became necessary. Children were listed as the only source of assistance when ill, going shopping or housekeeping was or became necessary to the elderly.

Examining the type of assistance most frequently provided by the elderly to the children, we do not find this population providing much of either instrumental or financial assistance to their children. Thirty-nine respondents said they never baby-sit for their grandchildren, while 17 said sometimes and 7 said rarely. Twenty-two indicated that this situation did not apply to them. Only 11 respondents provided some type of financial assistance to their children, with both the median and the mode falling on the "never" response. However, we find a very different picture in the "advice giving" category. When asked if they provide counseling to their children, the median was "sometime" and the mode was "always." Another question in this category asked how frequently the elderly helped their children with important decisions. If we combine the "always" and "sometime" response, 43 respondents helped their children make important decisions in their lives. When asked whether they provided some religious education for their grandchildren, 27 indicated either always or sometimes, while 26 said never and 12 said that it did not apply.

In the crisis interaction category, 20 respondents indicated that they had looked after a son or daughter when ill. Forty, however, said the question did not apply. Again, when asked how many had taken in an unemployed son or daughter, 21 responded affirmatively, either in the "always" or" sometime" response category, while 38 indicated that the question did not apply. Examining the affectionate component of the support system of the elderly, we find close affectionate relationships between the elderly and their children. When respondents were asked if their children had shown their love, 59 strongly agreed, while only 9 disagreed. Again, when asked if their children visited often, 42 said that their children visited often. When asked how often they talked to their children, 18 said very often, 35 said at least once a week, 7 said fairly often, 12 said never and 7 said it did not apply to them. When asked how often they sat down for meals with their children, 26 said very often, 27 said once a week, 6 said fairly often and 12 said never.

When asked how often they went out shopping with a daughter, as a joint leisure activity, 13 said very often, 22 said once a week, 12 said fairly often, 23 said never, and 11 indicated that it did not apply. When asked the same question but with a son, only 6 responded very often, 22 said once a week, ll said fairly often, 31 said never, 12 said it did not apply and 4 did not respond. Another set of questions dealt with remembering the elderly's birthday and wedding anniversary. When asked about the former, 27 respondents indicated that their children remembered very often, 19 said often, 8 said sometimes, 21 said never, 7 said it did not apply and 4 were missing. Less remembered wedding anniversaries, only 18 indicated very often, 5 said sometimes, and the rest either never remembered or it did not apply.

An examination of the relationship between the elderly and their *compadres* reveals that 40 respondents indicated that they have contact with their *compadres*, while 39 said no, 2 said some and 5 indicated it did not apply. It must be realized that since older Puerto Ricans in Hartford are relatively newcomers to the area, many of their *compadres* remained in Puerto Rico, as is indicated by the response to the question on whether their *compadres* lived nearby. Only 23 respondents had *compadres* who lived nearby and only 25 visit them often.

In conclusion, when the elderly respondents were asked what were the major responsibilities of adult children to parents, the most frequent response was to visit, the second most frequently given response was to love them and the third was to help whenever necessary. When asked what had changed the most in parent/adult children relations, 31 said respect for the older parent was no longer as important and significant as it had been when they were growing up; however, 45 still agreed that their children showed respect toward them, while 38 said they did not receive respect from their children.

PART III
The Support System of Older Hispanics Across Subpopulations

In the preceding section, the support system of older Puerto Ricans was discussed especially as it dealt with one primary com-

ponent of their informal support system, mainly that of their children
and grandchildren. In this section we examine the relationship, if
any, that ethnicity may have on the prevalence of the extended family
and the extent to which this structure provides an informal support
system of helping relationships among all Hispanic sub-populations in
the study.

Relying on language preference as one of many possible
indicators of the extent to which the populations under study have
acculturated or remain loyal to earlier patterns of language socialization, we examine English-Spanish preference among the four
sub-groups studied. Spanish was unanimously the languague of
preference for the Puerto Rican sub-group. Among South Texans it
was also almost unanimously chosen with 80 out of 84 respondents
listing Spanish as their language of preference, 3 chose English, and
one listed the "both" category. Among the San Antonio sample, 39
chose Spanish, 19 chose English and 40 chose both languages.
This was by far the most acculturated of the sub-populations if one
uses language preference as an indicator of acculturation. The New
Mexico sample fell in between the two categories, with 54 choosing
Spanish, 7 listing English, and l5 listing both languages.

In terms of family structure and household composition, the
four sub-populations were very similar. For example, as may be
expected the greatest number of respondents were widowed. Fifty-
five percent of the San Antonio sample, 51% of the Hartford sample,
63% of the New Mexico sample and 44% of the South Texas sample
were widowed. Again, similar to the situation of the Anglo elderly,
those who had a spouse at home were more likely to be younger and
males. For example, only 5 of the San Antonio women, 2 of the

Hartford, 2 of New Mexico and 5 of South Texas had a husband present at home. While of the men, 17 of the South Texas men and 2 respectively for each of the sub-poulations in the study had a wife present at home. The ratio of men to women in the study is about one third. Few had other members of the extended kin living with them which indicates that assumptions about the extended family in terms of a shared household are not valid for this population. For example, there were 3 respondents in the San Antonio sample who had a grandaughter living in the household and there were 5 South Texas respondents who listed a son as present in the household. This is about the same for all sub-samples in the study. Thus, if we are to test other aspects of the extended family structure, we must assume a modified extended family structure of the type noted by Sussman & Burchinal (1962). Only by examining informal kin support systems, especially as these deal with the immediate family, can we gauge the extent to which assumptions about traditional familism are applicable to this population of elderly.

Among the types of assistance most frequently needed and given to the elderly is transportation. The latter was given uniformly across sub-samples; however, the Puerto Rican sample received the most assistance from their children. As already noted, 30 Puerto Ricans received assistance from their children, while only 18 elderly from the San Antonio sample received assistance, 26 from New Mexico and 23 from South Texas. Social agencies were also important in providing assistance. As may be expected, more respondents received assistance from an agency in the San Antonio sample than in the other samples (n= 19). The New Mexico and South Texas samples received the least assistance with 8 and 10 respectively reporting this type of assistance. However, more elderly in these sub-populations reported that they provided their own transportation. Few respondents listed a spouse as providing assistance with transportation.

When respondents were asked who helped with household repairs, the Mexican-American sub-samples were more likely to list a son than the Puerto Ricans. However, we must be cautious with how this response is interpreted since no Puerto Ricans owned their homes while many in the other sub-samples did, therefore, the Puerto Ricans did not need this type of assistance from their children or other kin. Additionally, many of the men in the South Texas and New Mexico samples reported that they themselves took care of household repairs. Examining assistance with housekeeping, most respondents reported that they did not need assistance. When such help was necessary, however, daughters were given as the most likely response. For example, 11 of the San Antonio sample, 9 of the Hartford sample, 11 of the New Mexico sample and 10 of the South Texas sample listed their daughters as the ones who provided this type of help.

Whenever shopping assistance was necessary, again, it is daughters who are the most likely to help with this, 17 of the San Antonio, 19 of the Hartford, 16 of the New Mexico and 11 of the South Texas respondents listed their daughters.

One finding which strongly indicates the significance of the extended family for this group of elderly is the response given to the question, " Who cares for you when ill?" Only 7 respondents from a total sample of 347 listed a social agency with no respondent from South Texas choosing this option. While daughters were overwhelmingly the respondents' choice, sons were the second most frequently given response to this question. Thirty-eight of the San Antonio, 25 of the Hartford,16 of the New Mexico and 17 of the South Texas respondents listed their daughters as those who care for them when ill. However, 10 of the San Antonio, 16 of the Hartford, 14 of the New Mexico and 4 of the South Texas samples listed their sons. Many listed themselves as their caretakers when ill and there were a few dispersed answers listing in-laws (15), neighbors (12), nieces and nephews, (13) and spouses (14).

Other than self, children were listed again as those who were the most likely to assist when important decisions were made. Sixty-seven listed their daughters and 47 listed their sons as those who helped in these situations. Spouses were the fourth most frequent category with 21 respondents listing their spouses. Again, when asked about who assisted in legal matters and who helped them pay taxes, bills, etc., 42 respondents listed their daughters in response to the first question, while 39 listed their sons and 28 listed an agency. When responding to the second question, 50 listed their daughters, 29 listed their sons, and only 7 listed an agency.

Finally, another question which indicates the strength of the extended family has to do with how often they baby-sit for grand-children. Only 22 indicated that they always do; while 50 said sometimes, 45 said rarely, 138 said never, and 35 said it was not applicable. If we break down these responses by sites, we find very similar responses, 5 in the San Antonio sample, 7 in the Hartford sample, 4 in the New Mexico sample, and 6 in the South Texas sample said always, and 18 in the San Antonio, 6 in the Hartford, 15 in the New Mexico, and 11 in the South Texas samples responded sometime.

Conclusion

The focus of this chapter has been to reexamine traditional assumptions about the family structure of the Hispanic elderly with a special emphasis on the Puerto Rican sub-sample and across sub-population comparisons. Although the Puerto Rican sub-sample is the least acculturated of the sub-samples, following the acculturation scale employed in the larger study, a close examination of its family structure and patterns of kin support system does not indicate any significant variation between this sub-sample and other sub-samples in the study. Most of the elderly in all four sub-populations live alone, sometimes with a spouse and infrequently with children and/ or grandchildren. Thus, in terms of household composition as an indicator of extended familism, no differences are found between the Hispanic elderly and the dominant group. However, in patterns of assistance to include types and frequency of assistance by children, the elderly in the samples studied relied heavily on their children, but rarely on their grandchildren. Other members of the kin structure appear to provide assistance with greater frequency as are nieces and nephews, in-laws and spouses. Indeed, neighbors are much more likely to be of help to the elderly than are their grandchildren. This finding may be explained in terms of their grandchildren's ages. They may be too young to be of assistance to the elderly, since their affectionate ties appear to be much stronger. For example, grandchildren were mentioned frequently by the elderly as giving them love and happiness. However, if this were the case, and it can only be speculated here, we would expect the elderly to be of greater assistance to their children with baby-sitting. In parts II and III, it was indicated that respondents' children provided much instrumental assistance to the parents, however it was also documented that the elderly provided little baby-sitting assistance. Assuming an either-or situation, that is, either too young to help or older and not helping, the data reveal that the elderly in our sample do not have very close relationships with their grandhildren although they maintain great love for them.

Since another chapter in the book covers religiosity and religious beliefs for the studied populations, these variables are not investigated at length in this chapter. However, an exploratory examination of the relationship that may exist between variables that account for strength of religious convictions and frequency of attendance at religious services and indicators of family structure did not reveal a relationship between the two. That is, those who were the most religious do not seem to have a stronger kin support system nor for that matter were they more likely to educate their grandchildren in their religious beliefs. Thus, if religiosity, as operationalized in this study, is taken as a possible indicator of traditionalism, no relationships are found between its indicators and other indicators of extended familism, as operationalized in the study.

The above findings support the recent literature on the Hispanic elderly that raises questions concerning the applicability of traditional assumptions on extended familism to the current situation of this population of elderly. While our data show the strength of parent-child relationships, no similar strength is found in the grandparent-grandchild relationship which, if only speculative, suggests that the type of assistance provided by the current child cohort may not be available in a decade or so from now. The latter, of course, raises important issues concerning adjustments and changes that must be made in our present policy-making if it is going to address relevant issues for the 1990's.

Analysis of Scales Measuring Self-Esteem,Life Satisfaction and Mastery for Hispanic Elderly Populations

Robert D. Wrinkle, Hermila Anzaldua ,
and Delores Reed-Sanders,

One of the major problems in extending research from a majority community to a minority community is the question of the appropriateness of research instruments. Often researchers attempt to use research instruments with which they and the academic community are familiar and which are tested for a predominately majority community. Such instruments may or may not be appropriate for a minority community. This is a particularly vexing problem with regard to the nation's second largest minority group--Hispanics. Not only is the Hispanic population large and growing, but it is geo-graphically dispersed and distinct. Additionally, especially when considering the older Hispanic generation, there is often a language difference which intervenes. Thus, researchers who are interested in studying the Hispanic community often face several problems that majority community researchers do not. It is to this problem area that our study is directed.

The NHCoA (National Hispanic Counsel on Aging) study involved a large scale study of Hispanics in four geographical areas of the nation. The research instrument included a number of scales which were drawn from the existing literature in gerontology. These scales have been widely tested in the majority community. (Adams, 1969). In this study, they were applied to a particular part of a minority community--the Hispanic elderly.

This paper will analyze three widely used scales in terms of their applicability to this minority community. Our purpose is to ascertain the validity of these instruments for this population. Of course, the reliability of scales in any given population is sample dependent (Babbie, 1986).

Methodology

The sample design for the study of Hispanic elderly has been described earlier in this monograph. From the sample total, a usable sample of 347 respondents was drawn. Of this sample, 68.6% were female and 31.4% were male. Ages ranged from 62-years-old to 97-years-old, with a median age of 73 years. Most of the population was born outside the U.S.

The methodology used in this analysis was a relatively simple 2-step process and follows that of Adams (1969). First a factor analysis was done in an attempt to determine if the scales measure a single factor and to determine the components underlying in the scale. This technique was also used to determine how well the individual items of the scale correlate with the underlying factor. Factor analysis is particularly well suited for this purpose. A basic assumption of factor analysis is that the interrelationships between variables relate to a common or underlying factor. The technique manipulates the variables so as to disclose patterns of relationships, if any, extant among them. In essence. a variable's factor loading can be taken as the correlation between that variable and the underlying factor. The program used was FACTOR in SPSSX (Nie, et. al., 1975). As Adams did, we first used Principal Component Analysis (PCA) to identify the factors involved in the scale. An eigenvalue of 1.0 was set to produce the factors. The factors were then rotated to isolate "clusters" of highly related items.

The results of the factor analysis were used to identify component items of each scale and then a reliability analysis was performed on the scale. The reliability analysis measures how well the scale "holds together" in this population sample. Generally, the term reliability refers to three criteria:

1. a correlation between the same person's score at two different points in time;
2. the correlation between two different sets of items at the same time and
3. the correlation between the scale items for all persons who answer the items.

(Miller, 1983).

The program used was Reliability in SPSSX (Nie, et. al., 1975)., which allows for a means of evaluating additive item scales. The measure used was Chronbach's ALPHA, which is similar to the widely known reliabilit*y* coefficient KR-20 (Kuder Richardson-20). Essentially, Chronbach's ALPHA is the maximum likelihood estimate of the reliability coefficient if a parallel model is assumed to be valid. Generally speaking, the higher the ALPHA, the better the scale.

Findings
Life-Satisfaction

We first analyzed the Life-Satisfaction Index adapted from Adams (1969). This scale was developed in a study of an urban middle-class sample (Neugarten et al., 1961). It was later tested on a rural sample (Wood, Wylie & Sheafer, 1969) and a small town sample (Adams, 1969). Although both of these sampled elderly populations, they did not, however, sample minority populations. We tested the applicability of the LSI on our sample of Hispanic elderly. The 13 items included for analysis are as follows:

VAR 1: As I grow older, things seem better than I thought they would be;

VAR 2: I have gotten more of the breaks in life than most people I know;

VAR 3: This is the dreariest time in my life;

VAR 4: I am just as happy now as when I was younger;

VAR 5: These are the best years of my life;

VAR 6: Most of the things I do are boring or monotonous;

VAR 7: The things I do are as interesting to me as they ever were;

VAR 8: As I look back on my life, I am fairly well satisfied;

VAR 9: I have made plans for things I'll be doing a month or year from now;

VAR.10: When I think back over my life, I didn't get most of the important things I wanted;

VAR.11: Compared to other people, I get down in the dumps too often;

VAR 12: I have gotten pretty much what I expected out of life;

VAR 13: In spite of what people say, the lot of the average

person is getting worse, not better.

These items were scored on a 3-point basis of agree, don't

know and disagree. Neugarten et al. (1961) indicates that the Life

Satisfaction Index incorporates five components. Adams (1969)

notes these components as:

TABLE 1
Factor Loadings for Principal Component Analysis
of Life-Satisfaction Index

VARIABLE	FACTOR 1	FACTOR 2	FACTOR 3
Best years of life	.721	.284	-.282
Llife as happy as when young	.691	.125	-.366
Life as interesting as when young	634	.188	-.293
Life as expected	.624	.199	.422
Satisfied with life	.594	.064	.395
More breaks in life	.593	.206	.433
Life better than expected	.564	.149	.163
Planning ahead	.359	-.260	-.210
Average person getting worse	.144	.707	-.012
Fail to get important things	-.247	.540	-.417
Time is dreariest of lifeI	-.485	.384	.213
Life boring and monotonous	-.547	.285	.155
Get down in dumps often	-.667	.164	.067
Variance Accounted For	30.8%	10.4%	8.8%
Cumulative Variance	30.8%	41.2%	50.0%

1. zest for life as opposed to apathy;
2. resolution and fortitude as opposed to resignation;
3. congruences between desired and achieved goals;
4. high physical, social, and psychological self-concept
5. a happy mood-tone. (1969:470).

In our study, the Principal Components Analysis extracted three factors, accounting for 50% of the variance. The first factor was predominant, explaining some 30% of the variation. In this, our analysis is similar to that of Adams, who had one factor explain some 34% of the variance. Neither of the other two factors explains as much as 12% additional variance.

To identify more fully the components of this index for our sample, we performed a varimax rotated factor. The purpose of rotating the factors is to separate, as much as possible, the independent factors so as to locate "clusters" of highly related items (Adams, 1969; Nie, et. al.,1975).

The rotated factor matrix is presented in Table 2. As can be seen in this table, items VAR4 TO VAR7 and VAR11 load together. Adams (1969) found essentially the same pattern of factor loadings and identified this component as "Mood Tone." We follow Adams and also term Factor 1 as "Mood." The second factor includes loadings of items VAR1, VAR2, VAR8 and VAR12. Here our pattern of factor loadings diverges from that of Adams. Our Factor 2 incorporates portions of his Factors 2 and 3. The pattern of positive loadings of items such as: "*As I grow older, things seem better than I thought they would be;*" "*I have gotten more of the breaks in life than most people;*" "*As I look back on my life, I am fairly well satisfied;*" and "*I've gotten pretty much what I expected out of life*" indicates that this factor should be termed "Satisfaction."

Only two items load together on the third factor: "*In spite of what people say, the lot of the average man is getting worse, not better;*" and "*When I think back over my life, I didn't get most of the important things I wanted.*" Consequently, we have identified this factor as "Negativism." Adams' fourth factor was unnamed and included, as two of the three loaded items, our two items on factor 3.

Table 2
Factor Loadings for Varimax Rotation of Life-Satisfaction Index

VARIABLE	FACTOR 1 MOOD	FACTOR 2 SATIS- FACTION	FACTOR 3 NEGA- TIVISM
Life as happy as when young	.762	.215	.001
Best years of life	.740	.338	.132
Life as interest. as when young	.679	.250	.063
Planning ahead	.382	.006	-.308
Life better than expected	.311	.519	-.025
Life as expected	.183	.757	-.030
Satisfied with life	.168	.680	-.148
More breaks in life	.153	.747	-.018
Fail to get important things	.151	-.305	.641
Average person getting worse	-.036	.098	.714
Time is dreariest of life	-.465	-.049	.458
Life boring and monotonous	-.479	-.159	.387
Get down in dumps often	-.516	-.332	.315
Variance Accounted For	30.8%	10.4%	8.8%
Cumulative Variance	30.8%	41.2%	50.0%

Adams apparently was surprised by the loading of the third, more positive item.

Following the factor analysis, we performed a reliability analysis on the scale. The Life Satisfaction Index performed fairly well, with an ALPHA of .796. This high rating gives us assurance that, for our sample, the scale, "holds together." Only two items, both of which load on factor 3, seem to be candidates for exclusion, based on total item correlations.

Table 3
Reliability of Life-Satisfaction Index

VARIABLE	ITEM-TOTAL CORRELATION	SQUARED MULTPLE CORRELATION
Life better than expected	.439	.261
More breaks in life	.459	.307
Time is dreariest of life	.404	.202
Life as happy as when young	.560	.441
Best years of life	.573	.492
Life boring and monotonous	.448	.259
Life as interesting as when young	.501	.345
Satisfied with life	.474	.296
Planning ahead	.282	.113
Failed to get important things	.214	.119
Get down in dumps often	.564	.353
Life as expected	.487	.357
Average person getting worse	.134	.115

TOTAL ALPHA = .796

Adams indicated that there might be some gender-based difference with some items, we extended the analysis by dividing the sample by gender and repeating the reliability analysis. No significant differences emerged. The ALPHA for males was .781 and for females .802. Based on total item correlations, the same two items, *"In spite of what people say, the lot of the average person is getting worse, not better,"* and *"When I think back over my life, I didn't get most of the important things I wanted,"* are candidates for exclusion from the scale. By excluding these two items, the ALPHA would be marginally increased. Based on this analysis, application of the modified Life Satisfaction Index to an Hispanic Elderly population seems to be warranted.

Table 4
Factor Loadings for Principal Component
Factor Analysis of Mastery Index

VARIABLE	FACTOR 1	FACTOR 2
Often feel helpless	.748	.082
No way to solve problems	.726	-.110
Have little control	.722	-.254
Little I can do	.675	-.070
Feel pushed around	.663	-.151
Do just about anything	.285	.784
Future depends on me	.152	.825
Variance accounted for	37.3%	20.1%
Cumulative variance	37.3%	57.4%

Table 5
Factor Loadings for Varimax Rotation of Mastery Index

VARIABLE	FACTOR 1 MASTERY	FACTOR 2 EGO
Have little control	.759	-.096
No way to solve problems	.733	.045
Often feel helpless	.714	.238
Feel pushed around	.680	-.001
Little I can do	.674	.074
Do just about anything	.114	.826
Future depends on me	-.025	.838
Variance accounted for 37.3%		20.1%
Cumulative variance	37.3%	57.4%

Table 6
Reliability of Mastery Index

VARIABLE	ITEM-TOTAL CORRELATION	SQUARED MULTIPLE CORRELATION
No way to solve problems	.537	.377
Feel pushed around	.443	.296
Have little control	.498	.365
Do just about anything	.250	.221
Often feel helpless	.571	.363
Future depends on me	.145	.201
Little I can do	.474	.309

Total ALPHA = .712

Mastery

The second scale selected for analysis was Mastery, developed by Perlin, et al. (1978) and defined as the extent to which one regards one's own control in contrast to being fatalistically ruled. The scale has seven items, and includes:

VAR 1: There is really no way I can solve some of the problems I have;

VAR 2: Sometimes I feel that I'm pushed around in life;

VAR 3: I have little control over the things that happen to me;

VAR 4: I can do just about anything I really set my mind to do;

VAR 5: I often feel helpless in dealing with the problems of life.

VAR 6: What happens in the future depends mostly on me;

VAR 7: There is little I can do to change many of the important things in my life.

The items were scored on a 4-point basis of strongly agree to strongly disagree, and the resulting scores ranged from 7 to 28. Item scoring was reversed, where necessary, so that a high score indicated high mastery.

As before, the scale was first analyzed by means of Principal Component Factor Analysis. Two Factors emerged, explaining 37.3% and 20.1% of the variance respectively. When the factors were rotated in a varimax fashion, 5 of the seven factors loaded on factor 1. Only items 4 and 6 "*I can do just about anything I really set my mind to do,*" and "*What happens in the future depends mostly upon me,*" loaded on factor two. Consequently, we named Factor 1 "Mastery" and Factor 2, "Ego."

The reliability analysis produced an ALPHA of .712 for the scale, indicating a fairly high degree of reliability in the scale. Only the two items which loaded on factor two are candidates for exclusion from the scale.

Self-Esteem

Self-esteem is one of the major psychological concepts used to identify a person's conception of self-worth. In this research we rely upon the adaption by Perlin & Schooler of the Rosenberg self-esteem scale (Perlin & Schooler, 1978). This scale was constructed as a 10-item scale and included the following items:

VAR 1:   I feel that I'm a person of worth, at least on an
                equal plane with others;

VAR 2:   I feel that I have a number of good qualities;

VAR 3:   I take a positive attitude toward myself;

VAR 4:   On the whole, I am satisfied with myself;

VAR 5:   All in all, I am inclined to feel that I am a failure;

VAR 6:   I am able to do things as well as most people;

VAR 7:   I feel I do not have much to be proud of;

VAR 8:   I wish I could have more respect for myself;

VAR 9:   I certainly feel useless at times;

VAR 10: At times, I think I am no good at all.

These items were scored on a 4-point basis, from strongly agree, agree, disagree to strongly disagree.

We performed a Principal Component Factor Analysis on this scale and two factors emerged.

These two factors explain some 49.8% of the variation, with factor 1 explaining the great majority, 35.9%. Thus, it is apparent that

Table 7
Factor Loadings for Principal Components
Factor Analysis of Self-Esteem Index

VARIABLE	FACTOR 1	FACTOR 2
I have a positive self-attitude	.776	.189
I have a number of good qualities	.732	.286
I am satisfied with myself	.720	.236
I am a worthy person	.652	.252
I do things well	.614	.218
I have little self-respect	-.077	.751
I have little to be proud of	-.330	.349
I feel no good at times	-.514	.349
I am a failure	-.584	.379
I feel useless at times	-.638	.394
Variance accounted for	35.9%	13.9%
Cumulative variance	35.9%	49.8%

the first factor is the predominant underlying dimension of this scale.
Following Adams (1969) and Perlin & Schooler (1978), we then
performed a varimax rotation on the factors and the factor clusters
which emerged essentially resembled that of Perlin & Schooler. We
followed Perlin & Schooler and named factor 1 Self-esteem, and
factor 2 Self-Denigration. The two factors were sufficiently distinct
that Perlin & Schooler divided the factors and treated them as
different scales. Following Perlin & Schooler, we do also. The primary
difference is that our self-esteem scale is five items, (VAR1, VAR2,
VAR3, VAR4, and VAR6) and the self-denigration scale is four,
(VAR5, VAR8, VAR9 and VAR10). One item, VAR7 (*"I feel that I do*

Table 8
Factor Loadings for Varimax Rotation for
Factor Analysis of Self-Esteem

VARIABLE	FACTOR 1	FACTOR 2
I have a number of good qualities	.775	-.128
I have a positive self-attitude	.764	-.234
I am satisfied with myself	.740	-.165
I am a worthy person	.689	-.117
I do things well	.640	-.127
I have little self-respect	.317	.685
I have little to be proud of	-.106	.469
I feel no good at times	-.264	.562
I am a failure	-.309	.625
I feel useless at times	-.347	.665
Variance accounted for	35.9%	13.9%
Cumulative variance	35.9%	49.8%

not have much to be proud of"), was eliminated from both scales as it loaded on neither. We then performed reliability analyses on the Self-Esteem Scale and the Self-Denigration Scale.

In terms of reliability, the resultant self-esteem scale produced an ALPHA of .795, with all five items contributing.

The consistent item correlations (ranging from .50 to .65) indicate substantial agreement between the items and the scale. When we divided the sample into males and females, no significant differences emerged. The ALPHA for males was .780 and for females it was .803.

Table 9
Reliability of Self-Esteem Index

VARIABLE	ITEM-TOTAL CORRELATION	SQUARED MULTIPLE CORRELATION
I am a worthy person	.552	.347
I have a number of good qualities	.808	.439
I have a positive seld-attitude	.654	.490
I am satisfied with myself	.607	.429
I do things well	.502	.259

Total ALPHA=.795

Table 10
Reliability of Self-Denigration Index

VARIABLE	ITEM-TOTAL CORRELATION	SQUARED MULTIPLE CORRELATION
I am a failure	.489	.265
I have little self-respect	.265	.076
I feel useless at times	.602	.534
I feel no good at times	-.686	.588

Total ALPHA = .712

The results for the Self-Denigration scale were similar. The over-all ALPHA was .713, with one item (VAR.8-"*I wish I could have more respect for myself*") a strong candidate for exclusion. If this item were excluded, the resultant ALPHA would be .787. The overall ALPHA for males was .698 and for females,.864.

Discussion

This analysis of Life Satisfaction, Mastery and Self-Esteem scales in terms of a population of Hispanic elderly indicates that some modification of the scale items is required in order to apply these items to this population. As Miller (1983) has noted, all scales are sample dependent. What we have indicated here is that, for one limited study on a minority elderly population, the standard scales are useful, even though they require some modification. The results of this study suggest that these items should be considered for further application to samples of this population.

PART III:

Socio-Economic Implications on the Well-Being of Hispanic Elderly

The Health Status of the Hispanic Elderly

Marta Sotomayor and Suzanne Randolph

The rapid growth in the numbers of elderly Hispanics in this country raises concerns about their health condition and access to appropriate health care. While those who are 65 years of age and over comprise a small proportion of the present Hispanic population, their numbers are expected to grow faster than those of any other population group in this country; it numerically tripled in the last two decades. The numbers and rate of growth of elderly in the various sub-Hispanic populations vary. For example, half of the total population of elderly are of Mexican origin with its numbers growing at a rate of approximately double that of the Hispanic origin population as a whole (Special Population Reports, 1987). It is anticipated that by the year 2000, the 75-year-old and over group will grow considerably and will add to the already significant demands on available health resources (Development Associates, 1983).

Availability of Health Data on the Hispanic Elderly

While there are large amounts of data about the health status of the elderly in general, we know very little about the health of the Hispanic elderly. Overall, data on the health status of Latinos are limited and sparse; health related data on the elderly are even more limited.

The failure of most states to collect Hispanic specific vital statistics and health related information has been blamed for the lack of much needed information. Additional problems have been created by the neglect of health related data collection by agencies charged to do so and by the fragmentation of federal and state bureaucracies that often result in inadequate monitoring procedures and a poor quality of vital statistic records. "We do not know how many Hispanics die each year in this country, let alone their health status, unmet health care needs, or health care utilization rates" (Treviño, 1982).

Research on Latino elders is limited and rarely addresses the complex socio-economic problems that confront them and that often trigger serious and/or chronic health conditions. But, problems regarding Hispanic health data collection are much more complex than one would anticipate and often lead to questions related to the reliability and validity of available data. For example, data collection procedures have not considered the following factors:

1. health status variance among the different Hispanic sub-groups;
2. the differences between the health status of the various Hispanic populations and that of non-Hispanics;
3. differences that result from concentration of groups of Hispanic elderly in certain geographical regions of the country, thus contributing to stronger and continuous cultural influences on life styles and health care approaches;
4. the impact of the social, political, and economic forces over

long periods of time on their health status and use of health care resources;

5. methodological factors in data collection such as the lack of standardization of the categories used in soliciting racial/ethnic data, translation of instruments into the different colloquial styles of Spanish to accommodate different Hispanic groups, and the selection of research sampling methods that can generate a sufficient number of cases to allow for comparisons and generalizations.

Income and Educational Levels of the Latino Elderly

In general, the income levels of Hispanic families are lower than those for non-Hispanics. Their income and poverty levels showed a downward trend in the last 10 years (6.8%) which can vary for different age levels and from state to state. Twenty-two percent (22%) of the elderly live on incomes below the poverty level, of whom 39% are at the 125th percentile level (Bureau of the Census, 1983). Nearly one-quarter of all Hispanic households live in poverty (Bureau of the Census, 1984).

The formal years of education completed by this group of elderly are limited. For example, those 65 years of age and over reached a median of 7.1 years of school in 1985. But, only 21.1% of this group had completed high school. The Mexican origin elderly are 4 to 6 times more likely than the total population not to have completed 5 years of schooling. In fact, this group has the second highest illiteracy rate in the U.S. among racial/ethnic groups (Bureau of the Census, 1987).

There are indications that the Latino elderly have neither public nor private health insurance compared with the general population (Andersen, 1981; Lopez-Aquerez,1985). Health care, if accessible, is paid for the most part by Medicare and Medicaid and in the majority of cases is a commodity outside their immediate resources. One third of all Mexican-Americans do not see a physician in the course of a year (Moustafa & Weiss, 1968; Treviño & Moss, 1983) and there is no reason to believe that the elderly have more contacts with physicians than younger groups.

The Health Status of Poor Populations

As is the case with all poor people, economic conditions impinge on physical and emotional well-being. We know that stressful events and conditions have been associated with many forms of physical disorders and dysfunctions that often serve as triggering mechanisms for the onset of more serious physical and emotional problems. Unemployment and underemployment, limited income and support resources are known to lead to unsafe neighborhoods, less than desirable physical surroundings, sub-standard housing, and generally poor physical and mental health.

Available data indicate that poor people are hospitalized more frequently for longer periods of time, and receive more care at emergency rooms and out-patient departments than people with higher incomes. The scope of health care services is far narrower for low-income people than for those with an ability to pay. Those with little formal education are far more likely to report themselves as being disabled than are those who have higher educational levels. Low-income people receive less attentive individualized services and have more than three times as many bed disability days per person than people with higher incomes (Department of Health and Human Services, 1985).

A lifetime of poverty, the lack of education, the unavailability of health services all contribute to malnutrition and a higher number of chronic health problems that have led to the higher patterns of disability (partial and total) found among Hispanic elderly (Cantor & Mayer, 1976; DHHS, 1980 and 1985). Some regional studies point out that the incidence of disability among elderly Hispanics is significantly higher (about 25%) than for the general population (Juárez, 1984). This is in part a function of the unskilled occupational employment patterns of most Latinos during the course of their work history. The incidence of disability is much higher still for migrant and seasonal workers.

Some Health Data on Hispanic Elderly

A very limited number of studies have addressed issues in housing, mental health, utilization of services, political behavior, and death and dying. But, research on the health status of Latino elderly is even more sparse. A few studies that have taken place within the last five years are significant for they point out serious health indicators that place this population at high risk.

For example, a San Antonio, Texas, study among Mexican-American elderly found that 35% of the women and 45% of the men perceived their health as being "poor" (Gómez et al., 1973). The Colorado Interstate Research Associates study (1974) found that their sample participants mentioned a host of health problems; and the 1975 East Los Angeles Health Task Force study found that in the area of their study two out of every five Latino males aged 60 and over, and nearly one out of every two females of the same age, considered their health as being "poor" or "very poor". A South Texas study (Juárez, 1984) reported that more than two-thirds of both male and female Mexican-American elderly reported their health status as either "fair" or "poor". It is significant to note that Mexican-American elderly women seem to be the worst off in the South Texas study.

The Markides, et al., San Antonio study (1983) points out that Anglo males 60 years of age and over have a better health index score followed by that of Anglo females. Next in line are Mexican-American males, followed by what the authors believed to be the worst health status score, that of Mexican-American females.

Available data suggest that there are higher rates of cardiovascular disease and strokes, hypertension, diabetes, and obesity among Hispanic populations (DHHS, 1985). Diabetes, respiratory disease and hypertension afflict migrant farmworkers disproportionately and many also suffer from the effects of pesticide poisoning (Texas Health Coordinating Council, 1982).

Two of the available studies on the health status of this population group point out that cardiovascular disease is the leading cause of death among Mexican-Americans, just as it is among the rest of the population. But, a Texas study found a serious lack of even the most basic knowledge regarding the impact, nature, and control of cardiovascular disease among Mexican-American populations, a key prerequisite to adopting risk-reducing behaviors (Ramirez, 1981, American Heart Association, 1984). Both Mexican-Americans and their Anglo counterparts believed that it was "very important" to reduce their risk of this disease. But, over half of the

Mexican-Americans believed that they could not control their health through their own actions.

The American Heart Association study found that only about one-third of those interviewed had ever heard of the word "arterio-sclerosis" which describes the major biological process associated with cardiovascular disease. Hypertension was cited by only 13% of the Mexican-Americans as being associated with increased risk for cardiovascular disease. Eighty percent (80%) of the Anglo res-pondents could identify at least three behavioral habits or charac-teristics associated with increased risk of cardiovascular disease; while only 54% of the Mexican-Americans could do so.

A San Antonio study (Hazuda, et al., 1983) points out that Anglos are much better informed than Mexican-Americans from all socio-economic levels about heart attack prevention. Only one-third of the same respondents could name one or more of the warning signals of a heart attack, compared to more than half of the Anglo respondents. The findings suggest that certain cultural factors may be operating to account for differences over and above purely socio-economic factors. Mexican-American men ranked higher than women in their level of knowledge and prevention oriented behavior regarding dietary habits, blood pressure, cigarette smoking, and exercise, four risk factors related to hypertension. This same study made comparisons within specific neighborhoods that were fairly homogeneous in socio-economic status. Other studies support the same findings (Arlinger, 1982; Ramírez, Hernick & Weaver, 1981; Roberts and Lee, 1980).

The Purpose of the Study

This study sought to explore select health related areas among the Hispanic elderly including:

1. perceived health status;

2. health problems as barriers to daily functioning; and

3. informal and formal support in time of need.

Data were collected in four cities, two of which are classified as rural and two as metropolitan areas. One city, McAllen, Texas, is contiguous to the Mexican border; thus, cultural norms, values, beliefs, and language are being renewed by continuous interchanges. One area, Northern New Mexico, traces its Hispanic roots to the early 1500's, yet the Spanish language and culture are retained particularly by the elderly population. These two geographical areas claim the highest number of Hispanic elderly over the age of 65 years.

The San Antonio, Texas, data reflect primarily a Mexican-American elderly population that, while in the city for several generations, also maintains cultural and language patterns relatively well, despite considerable cultural interchange with the Anglo population. The data from Hartford, Connecticut, allow for comparison with a Puerto Rican population of elderly, most of whom have been in this country for considerable time, but maintain a strong affiliation with their language and culture.

The Findings of the Study

The findings of this study allowed for comparisons in terms of Hispanic sub-groups, geographical location, and degree of interchange with the Anglo community.

The following results are based on a sample of 101 respondents. An over-arching research question in this study was the
extent to which self-rated health was related to other health variables.
Self-rated health was measured by responses to the question: "How
would you rate your health at the present time?". Possible responses
included: "excellent," "good," "fair," "poor," and "very poor." For the
purposes of this report, a new variable was created, yielding only two
groups--those who responded excellent or good were collapsed into
one group ("good health") and those who responded fair, poor, or
very poor were collapsed into the second group ("poor health"). Most
of the sample (72%) were in the poor health group (n=80).

The health status indicators included: number of bed disability days, perceived need for medical care, reported changes in
health status over five years, and self perceptions of health problems
as barriers to personal functioning.

Daily functioning was measured by respondents' reports of
need for assistance with the Activities of Daily Living (ADL) and
Instrumental Activities of Daily Living (IADL). In particular, respondents were asked if they could perform the activity without help,
with some help, or were completely unable to perform the activity.
The need for help or complete inability to perform the activity were
regarded as need for assistance. The ADL included: walking, bathing,
getting in or out of bed or chair (transfer), dressing, eating, and
keeping one's appeareance. The IADL included: shopping, meal
preparation, transportation, housework, telephone use, money
management, and taking medicines.

Informal support in time of need was measured by a number
of questions related to respondents' reliance on family, friends, and

agency resources for assistance with the ADL and IADL. In addition
to questions about who helps with ADL and IADL, respondents were
also asked how often they got help.

Descriptive statistics were generated for each variable and
examined for patterns of response. In addition, to investigate the
association between self-rated health status and other variables,
contingency table analyses were used where appropriate, with the
chi-square statistic subjected to testing at the 95 percent level of
confidence.

Heath Status
A. Bed Disability Days

Responses to two questions were used to examine this
health indicator. The first question dealt with the number of days in
the last six months respondents were so sick that it interfered with
their usual daily activities. Only 43% reported that they were never
that sick. The other 57% reported frequencies ranging from less than
one week to over six months. When asked how many days they were
hospitalized, two-thirds (66%) said "none" even though, as indicated
above, over half were so sick that it interfered with their daily activities
from a week to six months. One fourth were in the hospital 1-2 weeks;
10% were in more than 2 weeks.

B. Perceived Need for Medical Care

Overall 27% felt a need for medical care. Nearly a third of
those who reported their health as being fair to very poor indicated
that they felt a need for medical care. Only 14% of those who rated
their health as good to excellent reported that they felt a need for

medical care.

Table 1
Descriptive and Chi-Square Statistics for Selected
Health Status Indicators by Self-Rated Group(1)

Health Indicator	Percentage Responding			
	Good Health n=31	Poor Health n=80	Total	X2(df)
1. Bed Disability Days				n.s.
a. Never	56	37	43	
b. Less than 1 week	24	19	20	
c. 2 to 3 weeks	15	26	23	
d. 1 to 6 months	6	19	15	
2. Hospital Days				n.s.
a. None	71	63	66	
b. 1 to 2 weeks	17	27	24	
c. More than 2 weeks	12	10	10	
3. Need for Medical Care				
(%yes)	14	322	27	n.s.
4. Change in Health Status				
a. Better	21	8	12	9.83(2)*
b. Some	59	41	46	
c. Worse	21	51	42	
5. Health Problems as Barriers				16.54(2)**
a. Never	50	20	29	
b. Some	41	35	36	
c. A Lot	9	45	35	

1 Some percentages total more than 100, because of rounding.
* $p < .01$
** $p < .001$

C. Change in Health Status

Respondents were asked if their health was worse, better, or the same as five years ago. Some 42% reported that their health had worsened while the other 58% said that their health was about the same or better. There was a significant difference between those who rated their health as fair to very poor and those who rated their health as good to excellent ($X2(2)=9.83$, p <.01). Over half (51%) of the fair to poor group said their health had "worsened," whereas over three fourths (79%) of the good to excellent group said their health was "the same or better."

D. Health Problems as Barriers

In a related item, respondents were asked how much their health problems stood in their way of doing the things they liked. Most said "some" (36%) or "a lot" (35%). Another significant difference emerged between the poor health and good health groups ($X2(2)= 16.54$, p < .001). Among the poorhealth group, 45% said that their health problems stand in the way "a lot," while only 9% of the good health group said so. In contrast, half of the good group said health problems never stand in their way, while only a fifth of the poor health group said "never."

E. Other Health Status Indicators

Respondents were asked other series of questions regarding care they received when ill, including by whom and how often. They were also asked about any accidents they had had lately, the nature of the accidents, and their ability to call for help.

Regarding care they received when ill, 78% said they have someone who can care for them when ill. There were similar percentages in both the poor health and good health groups (77% and 78%, respectively). The most frequently reported helper was identified as an adult child (48%). Of these, most were daughters (33%). Nearly 30% reported that they help themselves.

Few other helpers were identified: 11% reported other relatives (in-laws, niece/nephew, grandchildren); 4% reported neighbors or friends; and 5% reported that a spouse cared for them. Only 2% reported that they are cared for by someone from a formal agency. In terms of how often they were helped, percentages were similar for those reporting "daily" (24%), "several times per year" (28%), or "as necessary" (25%).

Regarding accidents, only 12% reported that they had had an accident lately. The percentages were similar for both the poor health and good health groups. Of those who did report having an accident, three percent or less reported falls resulting in an injury or auto accidents. Also among those who had an accident over two-thirds (68%) said they were able to call someone for help (70% in the poor health group, 63% in the good health group). When asked who helped them during the accidental injury, most reported "no one" (23%). "Other" was the next most frequently reported (19%), but of those specifically identified, there were tied percentages for ("daughter" and "agency persons" (15% each). "Spouses," "sons," and "grand-daughters" were each reported by 7% of the respondents. "Neighbors" were the least reported group (4%).

F. Functioning

The results in this section are reported separately for Activities of Daily Living (ADL) and Instrumental Activities of Daily Living (IADL). These two sets of data are similar to those collected in previous national studies of the elderly population in the United States.

Table   2

Descriptive and Chi-Square Statistics by Self-Rated Health Group or
Reported Assistance with Illness, Accidents and Assistance
with Accidental Injury*

Variable	Percentage Reporting			
	Good Health N=31	Poor Health N=80	Total	X2(df)
1. Has someone who can care for them when ill (% yes)	78	77	77	n.s.
Who helps You?				n.s.
a. Daughter	32	33	33	
b. Son	13	16	15	
c. Self	36	27	30	
d. Spouse	7	4	5	
e. Other Relative	7	12	11	
f. Friend,Neighbor	3	4	4	
g. Formal Agency	2	3	2	
2. Recent Accident (% yes)	14	11	12	n.s.
3. Type of Accident/Injury				n.s.
a. Fall with Broken Bone(s)	5	6	6	
b. Automobile	4	2	6	
c. Other	9	11	10	
4. Able to Call for Help with Accident (% yes)	63	70	68	n.s.
5. Who Called for Help with Accidental Injury:				n.s.
a. Daughter	13	17	15	
b. Son	0	11	8	
c. Self	50	11	23	
d. Spouse	13	6	8	
e. Grandchild	0	11	8	
f. Friend/Neighbor	0	6	4	
g. Formal Agency	25	11	15	
h. Other	0	28	19	

* Some percentages total more than 100 because of rounding

Table 3
Percentages for Respondents' Reports of Degree of Assistance
Needed with ADL by Self-Rated Health Group (1, 2)

Activity	Good Health		Poor Health		Total	
	Percentage Reporting					
	Some Help	Completely Unable	Some Help	Comp. Unable	Some Help	Comp. Unable
1. Eating	13	0	18	1	16	1
2. Dressing	13	3	24	1	21	2
3. Appearance	13	0	22	3	20	2
4. Walking	19	0	30	1	27	1
5. Bed/chair Transfer	16	0	23	3	21	2
6. Bathing	13	6	23	4	20	5

1. Percentages are reported only for those respondents who said they need "some help" or were "completely unable" to do the activity alone.
2. None of the chi-square statistics were significant.

G. ADL

Table 3 shows percentages of respondents who reported that they need some help or were completely unable to perform the ADL functions asked about in this study. In order of frequency (most to least reported), respondents reported that they need some help with or were completely unable to perform the following ADL: walking (28%), bathing (25%), getting in or out of a bed or chair tied with dressing oneself (23%) each), keeping one's appearance (22%), and eating (17%). There were no significant differences in reported need for ADL assistance between the poor health and good health groups. Six percent or fewer of the respondents reported that they were completely unable to perform any of the ADL.

H. IADL

Table 4 displays percentage data for responses to the traditional IADL items. Noticeably, the percentages of respondents reporting that they needed IADL assistance was higher than those for ADL assistance. In order of frequency (most to least reported), there was a tie for first between telephone use and shopping (44% each).

Table 4
Percentages for Respondents' Reports of Degree of Assistance
Needed with IADL by Self-Rated Health Group (1)

Activity	Percentages Responding					
	Good Health		Poor Health		Total	
	Some Compl		Some Compl		Some Compl	
	Help	Unable	Help	Unable	Help	Unable
1. Telephone use a	23	0	40	12	35	9
2. Shopping b	23	3	39	13	34	10
3. Meal Preparation	26	3	26	20	26	15
4. Housework	17	3	33	20	28	15
5. Taking Medicines	17	0	28	5	25	4
6. Money Management	10	10	27	10	22	10

1. Percentages are reported only for those respondents who said
   they need "some help" or were "completely unable" to do the
   activity alone.
aX2(df) = 8.13(2), p < .05
bX2(df) = 6.24(2), p < .05
cX2(df) = 9.55(2), p < .01

These were followed by housework (43%), meal preparation (41%), money management (32%) and taking medicines (29%).

Significant differences were found for three of the IADL, with higher percentages of the poor health group than the good health group reporting need for help with telephone use, shopping, and housework. For telephone use, 52% of the poor health group reported need for assistance (including 12% who were completely unable to perform the activity), while only 23% of the good health group with no one completely unable, reported a need for help ($X2(2)=8.13$, p <.05). For shopping, a similar percentage difference was found (52% of the poor health group reported need for help with 13% completely unable), compared to 26% (with 3% unable) for the good health group ($x2(2) = 6.24$, p <.05). The percentage difference was also similar for housework: 53% of the poor health group reported a need for help with 20% completely unable, compared to 20% (with 3% unable) of the good health group ($X2(2) = 9.55$, p <.01).

Table 5
Percentages of Respondents Reporting that They Get Help with ADL, IADL, and Other Activities by Health Group (1, 2)

Activity	% Responding Yes Get Help (3)		
	Poor Health	Good Health	Total
1. ADL	62	43	57
2. Transportation	83	81	82
3. Housekeeping	69	54	65
4. Shopping	78	67	75
5. Money Management	70	62	67
6. Household Repairs	64	61	63
7. Automotive Repairs	37	45	40
8. Legal Aid	66	56	64
9. Important Decision-Making	72	72	72

1. The ADL were asked about in a single question.
2. The only IADL asked about were transportation, housekeeping, shopping and money management.
3. There were no statistical differences between the health groups.

Informal and Formal Support in Time of Need

It appears that respondents have a good deal of support available with ADL and IADL. Table 5 displays percentage data for respondents' reports of help received with ADL and IADL. The largest percentage of respondents received help with transportation (82%), followed by shopping (75%), money management (67%), and housekeeping (65%). The least reported activity with which they received help was car repair (40%). There were no statistical differences between the health groups.

As shown in Table 6, much of this assistance is provided by adult children (primarily daughters) for all activities. Across all respondents, less than 10% reported that their spouse provided assistance with activities. However, in the good health group spouses provided assistance with ADL (16%), making important decisions (11%), money management (11%), transportation (10%), and car repairs (10%). Significant others (grandchildren, in-laws, other relatives, friends and neighbors) were reported most as providing help with transportation (10%), household repairs (14%), and shopping (14%).

Though not statistically significant, some differences between the poor health and good health groups were of interest. Specifically, among the poor health group the most frequently reported helpers were adult children for transportation, house repairs, making important decisions, and handling legal matters. Among the good health group, for those same activities, respondents stated that they performed the activity without help. It also appears that informal helpers provide support quite frequently. The highest percentage of respondents reported that they received assistance with transportation and

Table 6
Percentages of Helper Types Reported by Respondents
Across Health Groups (1)

Activity	Percentage Reporting		
	Daughter/Son	Spouse	Other
1. ADL	43	9	0
2. Transportation	33	5	19
3. Housekeeping	19	6	12
4. Shopping	34	6	14
5. Money Management	30	9	11
6. Household Repairs	31	5	14
7. Automotive Repairs	33	9	7
8. Legal Aid	40	3	10
9. Important Decision-Making	42	8	10

1. Chi-square statistics testing the association between health groups and helper type were not significant.

housekeeping daily (24% and 36%, respectively) or several times a week (26% and 28%, respectively). Shopping assistance was reportedly provided weekly (43%) and assistance with money management was reportedly provided monthly (49%). Assistance with legal matters was provided as necessary (52%), and support was reportedly provided several times a year for making important decisions (14%), house repairs (33%), and auto repairs (31%). Four percent or fewer of the respondents reported that they never received assistance with any of the activities. These trends did not differ by health groups.

Formal Helpers

In addition to the informal helpers reported above, some respondents also reported that they received assistance with ADL,

IADL, and other activities from social agencies. Table 7 displays percentage data for respondents' reports of assistance from these agencies by health group. Although "social agency" was a response category included among the helper types previously reported, a separate table was generated to highlight the data. As reported earlier, there were no significant differences found for the association between helper type and health group.

Of note, however, are the data in Table 7 which suggest that respondents most frequently reported assistance from formal helpers with household repairs (19%), transportation (18%), and legal aid (14%). Very few respondents (6% of less) reported assistance from formal helpers for any of the other activities. The frequency of

Table 7

Percentage of Respondents Reporting that They Receive Help from Formal Agencies for Assistance with ADL, IADL, and other Activities by Health Group (1)

Activity	Percentage Responding		
	Poor Health	Good Health	Total
1. ADL	3	6	4
2. Transportation	16	20	18
3. Housekeeping	7	4	6
4. Shopping	3	4	4
5. Money Management	4	0	3
6. Household Repairs	22	11	19
7. Automotive Repairs	7	0	4
8. Legal Aid	12	19	14
9. Important Decision-Making	4	0	3

1. Chi-square statistics testing the association between health groups and helper type were not significant.

assistance provided was reported as: "several times a week" (33%) or
"as necessary" (24%) for household repairs; "several times a week"
(26%) or "daily" (24%) for transportation; and "as necessary" (52%) for
legal aid.

Discussion

The data presented here highlight the debilitating health
conditions found among these two groups of Latino elderly that
inevitably have an negative impact on their quality of life and life
satisfaction. Over one-half of the study participants indicated that
their poor health interfered with doing the things they liked best.
One-fourth reported being hospitalized during the previous year; with
close to one-half reporting that their health had worsened during the
previous five years. Further, their condition was debilitating enough
to require help with basic day-to-day activities. It is significant to note
that only 2% had received care from someone representing an
agency. But equally as important, as it pertains to informal supports
available to them, the majority had someone who could care for them;
usually a family member.

These findings also speak to the relationship between the
discrimination experienced throughout the life-span by minority of
color elderly and its effects on their use of available health resources,
or the "double jeopardy" hypothesis. Specifically, this hypothesis
posits that being old and a member of a minority of color group places
an individual in a doubly disadvantaged position (Jackson, 1978).

Findings that support this hypothesis are inconclusive
primarily due to methodological issues. For example, while the Dowd
& Bengtson, (1978) and Jackson (1978) studies supported the

double jeopardy hypothesis, the Ward (1983), and Markides (1981 and 1983) studies did not. At the heart of these opposite positions, lies the issue of subjective (measured by respondents' perceptions of their own health) versus objective (assessments of health status by a physician or by standard rating instruments) methods. But, there are really no entirely satisfactory objective measures of health (Shanas & Maddox (1985), or subjective measures for that matter. The argument has been made that findings based on a single measure of health status should be interpreted with caution (George & Bearon, 1980). These two factors, subjectivity and objectivity, are in reality inextricably related.

To get a clear understanding of the circumstances that lead to the present health condition experienced by Hispanic elderly, the following factors will have to be considered: sex, age, economic and class factors, level of education, ability to communicate in English with health-care providers, date of immigration to this country, generational position in the continuum of migration, proximity to the mother country and/or culture, degree of acculturation or adaptation to the new culture, as well as ethnicity or race. All of these factors have an impact on their ability to access and use available health care services. All of these factors play a part in selecting the coping armamentarium that allow elderly of Hispanic descent to survive in what has been labeled "a hostile environment".

An approach that takes into consideration a "multidimen-sional conceptualization of health status and its relationship with life-satisfaction and the specific functions of coping" (Lohr, et al., 1988) will certainly contribute to the understanding of the Hispanic elderly, their health condition and how they cope with the daily process of living.

An Examination of the Economic Support Systems of Elderly Hispanics

Alejandro Garcia

The intent of this paper is to examine the economic status of elderly Hispanics. In order to do so, a number of factors are examined, including work history, employment status, income sources, private and public pension coverage. Elderly Hispanics are more than twice as poor as White elderly for a variety of reasons. They receive limited benefits from Social Security and Old Age Insurance program; they have a history of unskilled employment which had no private pension coverage, no savings, and an inability to depend on family for financial support.

Introduction

Hispanic elderly are in economic crisis brought on by a number of factors beyond their control. Their poverty rate has been gradually reduced from 28 percent in 1975 to 24 percent in 1985. However, that rate is still over twice as high as the poverty rate for White elderly (11 percent in 1985). See Table 1 below.

It should be noted that poverty rates are questionable indicators of the extent of poverty. The food plan used in calculating the poverty index "was originally designed for emergency periods only and no one is expected to have to live over a long period of time on these very minimal food amounts. This implies that these food diets would be detrimental to your health" (Schulz, 1976). It is interesting to note that the poverty threshold is only used to measure poverty. This author knows of no public assistance program which meets or exceeds the poverty threshold. Most of these programs only meets a percentage of need as determined by a number of measures. Many benefit programs reflect conflicts regarding adequacy of benefits versus concern with disincentives to work.

Table 1
Poverty Rates for Persons Age 65 and Over - 1975 to 1985

Year	White	Black	Spanish Origin
1985	11%	32%	24%
1980	14%	38%	26%
1975	13%	36%	28%

Source: Table 16, Current Population Reports, Bureau of the Census, P60/154, 1985.

In examining the poverty rates for elderly Hispanic men and women, it was found that the rates were higher for women (27.4%) than for men (19.1%). In comparing Hispanics with whites, the data in Table 2 indicates that poverty rates for elderly White men (6.9%) and women (13.8%) are lower.

Findings from the National Hispanic Council on Aging (NHCoA) tend to validate these findings. In the NHCoA study, 23 percent of elderly Hispanic males and 27.6 percent of females had

Table 2
Poverty Rates for Persons Age 65 and Over by Sex, Race and Spanish Origin (1985)

Sex	White %	Black %	Spanish Origin %
Male	6.9	26.6	19.1
Female	13.8	34.8	27.4

Source: Current Population Reports, U.S. Bureau of the Census, P60/154, 1985.

income under $4,000, while 63.2 percent of males and 73.6 percent of females in the same ethnic sub-group had incomes of less than $6,000.

Briggs (1977) suggests that "residual cultural factors" have tended to keep Hispanic women in the home raising children and out of the work force. The literature has suggested that the Hispanic family, because of its larger size and need for the mother to provide child care, has more rigorously adhered to the traditional gender roles, i.e. women work as wife and mother, as opposed to outside worker. However, this interpretation is contradicted by findings reported by Gómez, Martin and Gibson (1976) who found that among an elderly sample of Mexican-American women, 52 percent of the respondents had reported early work histories by age 16, primarily in domestic and migrant labor jobs. It is quite possible that these types of work experiences, i.e., domestic and farmwork, were interrupted by child birth, not documented in any kind of labor force participation statistics and not covered by social security.

The higher poverty rate of elderly Hispanic women, as

compared to their male counterparts, may also be due to loss of available income because of health costs and early death of spouse. In essence, the elderly Hispanic female is less financially prepared to face old age than her counterpart non-Hispanic white female due to types of employment held by herself or spouse, limited or non-participation in the work force plus cultural variables that reinforce a more traditional feminine role.

The Elderly Hispanic Family

There are a number of myths surrounding the relationship of Hispanic families to their elderly. These myths range from a traditional perspective which says that elderly parents are the responsibility of their children ("*el deber de los hijos son los padres*") to a modern perspective which asserts that this is no longer the case with elderly Hispanic parents expecting less support from their children and greater support from the government.

In studying traits of Mexican-American families, María Zúñiga Martínez (1979), found that "Mexican culture emphasizes the primacy of the family..." She describes this culture as being "family oriented, extended versus nuclear and quite intradependent." She argues that, in spite of studies in Los Angeles and San Antonio which found a very small percentages of extended family households, Mexican-Americans still adhere "to the extended family concept as reflected in *barrios* where kin live next door, either on the same block, or a short walking distance from one another, and thus, operationalize the concept of support and intradependence." Grebler et al., (1970) suggested that "the living arrangements, visiting patterns, and relationships within the extended kinship group have declined in importance with increased urbanization, accultu-ration, and contact with the dominant system."

Zúñiga Martínez (1979) also found that support of the elderly in the areas of health care, emotional support, daily living aid, and economic support "were perceived within the domain of the family". It should be noted that this perception may be at variance with reality, even though the intent may be present. Even if relatives of Hispanic elderly want to help, there is question about whether they are financially able to do so. Census data available from 1985 show that the poverty rate for all Hispanics in 1985 was 29 percent (up slightly from 28.4 percent in 1984). This is a higher poverty rate than that for elderly Hispanics who only had a poverty rate of 24 percent. As can be seen in Table 3 below, poverty rates for blacks and non-Hispanic whites declined slightly between 1984 and 1985, but the poverty rate for Hispanics actually increased slightly.

Table 3
Percentage of Poverty Rates by Race and Spanish Origin

	Poverty Rate	
	1985 %	1984 %
Spanish Origin	29	28.4
White	11.4	12
Black	31.3	33.8

Source: Current Population Reports, U.S. Bureau of the Census. P60/154, 1985.

Data from 1982, that provides poverty rates according to age group, also support the point of view that relatives of poor elderly

Hispanics themselves tend to be poor and unable to provide financial support to their elderly relatives. As can be seen in Table 4 below, the poverty rate for Hispanics below the age of 25 is 33 percent, about one-third higher than it is for elderly Hispanics, with only those in the age groups of 45 to 64 having a substantially lower poverty rate than do elderly Hispanics.

It is possible that, rather than the elderly being dependent on their non-elderly relatives for support, the reverse may be the case due to the fact that the younger Hispanics may be more subject to the vicissitudes of the work force. The elderly, on the other hand, may have limited but stable incomes and be more likely to own homes, even though these may be substandard. Such a pheno-menon need not be seen as extraordinary, but as one more manifestation of family intradependence.

Table 4
Poverty Rate for Spanish-Origin Persons By Age

Age	Poverty Rate %
Under 25 years	33
25 to 34	23
35 to 44	26
45 to 54	18
55 to 64	17
65 and over	25

Source: Current Population Reports, P60/134, 1982.

Sources of Income

In order to obtain a more complete picture of economic resources available to elderly Latinos, a review of sources of income is important. As noted in Table 5, social security benefits (not public assistance) accounted for a larger percentage of Hispanic elderly's income (44%) than it did for all elderly (38%). In addition, personal earnings accounted for 22 percent of Hispanic elderly's income, as opposed to only 16 percent for all elderly. On the other hand, assets income accounted for 28 percent of all elderly's income, while it only accounted for 12 percent of Hispanic elderly's income. Also of particular importance is the fact that Latino elderly were more dependent on public assistance for part of their income (10% than were all elderly (3%).

The National Hispanic Council on Aging study found that 30 percent of elderly Hispanic males and 33.7 percent of elderly

Table 5
1984 Sources of Income For All Elderly and Hispanic Elderly

Sources of Income	Aged Units	
	All %	Hispanics %
Social Security	38	44
Other Pensions	14	12
Earnings	16	22
Assets Income	28	12
Other, Including public assistance	3	10

Source: Social Security Administration. Unpublished Data, 1987.

Hispanic females had social security old age insurance benefits as their only source of income, while an additional 31.9 percent of the males and 34.9 percent of females in this group had both old age insurance and SSI as sources of income. Only 8 percent of elderly Hispanic males and 9.6 percent of elderly Hispanic females said that they depended solely on SSI for income (an additional 4.3 males and 5.6 percent females in this group said that they received "welfare", but it was not clear what source was being mentioned).

Only 2.9 percent of elderly Hispanic males and 1.2 percent of elderly Hispanic females in the NHCoA study reported receiving income from employment and old age insurance. This contradicts data collected under the same study which showed that 16 percent of males and 7.7 percent females in this group reported that they were still employed.

Importance of Social Security Benefits

As can be seen in Table 6, only 3 out of 4 elderly Hispanics were receiving social security benefits in 1984, while 9 out of 10 elderly overall received such benefits (91%). This low level of coverage tends to be reflective of intermittent work patterns and a history of agricultural and other non-covered employment. Hispanic elderly were found to be considerably more dependent on social security than were all elderly. Thirty-eight percent of elderly Hispanics depended on social security for 90 percent of more of their income. While only 24 percent of all elderly had such a level of dependence on this income source. It is also mportant to note that over one-fourth (27%) of elderly Hispanics depended solely on social security for their income, while this was the case for only 14

Table 6
Importance of Social Security for All Elderly and Hispanic Elderly (1984)

Percent of Aged Unit	Aged Units	
	All %	Hispanic %
With Social Security	91	76
Proportion of Income from		
Social Security Beneficiary		
Units		
50% or more	62	72
90% or more	24	38
100%	14	27

Source: Social Security Administration. Unpublished Data, 1987.

percent of the elderly overall. In other words, there were lower percentages of elderly Hispanics receiving social security old age insurance benefits, but those who did receive it had a greater dependence on this source of income as their sole, or major source, than did the elderly in general. Data from the National Hispanic Council on Aging study had a higher rate of elderly Hispanic respondents dependent solely on old age insurance benefits (30% males and 33.7% females).

Dependence on Retirement Pensions Other than Social Security

Overall, Social Security Administration data showed that 38 percent of the elderly had a pension supported either by private or public funds, while this was the case for only 20 percent of Latino elderly. Sixteen percent of all elderly held a pension financed by public funds, while only 7 percent of Hispanic elderly did so. Twenty-four percent of all elderly held private pensions, while only 13 percent of Hispanic elderly did so. The NHCoA study found a similar rate of elderly Hispanics with pensions supported by private sources (12.3%). These findings reflect the fact that Hispanic elderly

Table 7
Dependence on Retirement Pensions Other than Social Security

Source	Aged Unit	
	All %	Hispanic %
Total	38	20
Other Public Pensions	16	7
Private Pensions	24	13

Source: Social Security Administration. Unpublished Data, 1987.

tend to be employed in agricultural and other unskilled employment which carries limited or no pension coverage. Even if such programs carried some type of pension coverage, elderly Hispanics may still not benefit extensively due to the fact that they are the last hired and the first fired, therefore no able to obtain vesting rights. In addition, most of these programs for low income workers would not provide portability of plans.

Receipt of Social Security and SSI

Social Security Administration (SSA) data show that Hispanic elderly tended to be more dependent on SSI than did the elderly overall. Slightly over one-fourth (26%) of elderly Hispanics received SSI compared to 8 percent of the elderly population overall. There were higher percentages of Hispanic elderly receiving SSI with and without social security than was the case for all elderly. The NHCoA study found a higher percentage of elderly Hispanic males (31.9%) receiving SSI and social security than did the SSA findings. The Social Security Administration data and the National Hispanic Council on Aging data tend to agree in finding that approximately one out of 8 elderly Hispanic males (12%) were receiving SSI without social security. In addition, the SSA data showed hat 12% of Hispanic elderly (versus 7% of all elderly) received neither social security nor SSI. It is speculated that this is the case because there may still be

Table 8
Receipt of Social Security and SSI for
All Elderly and Hispanic Elderly (1984)

Source	Aged Unit	
	All %	Hispanics %
Social Security and no SSI	85	62
SSI	8	26
with no Social Security	6	14
w/o Social Security	2	12
Neither Social Security nor SSI	7	12

Source: Social Security Administration. Unpublished Data, 1987.

some barriers to Latino elderly applying for services due to language difficulties, discrimination, fear, self-selecting out, and so forth.

Social Security's Role in Reducing Poverty:

Of those persons receiving social security, there was a 50 percent higher rate of Hispanic elderly who were poor than the elderly overall (20% versus 14% poverty rates) See Table 9.

Table 9
Social Security's Role in Reducing Poverty

Family Income Status	OASDI Beneficiaries	
	All %	Hispanics %
Poor	14	20
Poor Without Social Security	50	57
Difference	36	37

Source: Social Security Administration. Unpublished Data. 1987.

If one tried to determine what impact Social Security had in removing the elderly from poverty, the poverty rate would be increased to 50 percent for all elderly and to 57 percent of Hispanic elderly. In other words, social security benefits, for a variety of reasons, did not have a disproportionate effect in removing elderly Hispanics from poverty. Further analysis regarding benefit levels would suggest that lower benefit levels for elderly Hispanics is a major reason for the limited effect that social security has in reducing poverty among Hispanic elderly.

Because of past work history in the areas of agriculture and unskilled labor, Hispanics were found to receive lower benefit

levels than did non-Hispanic whites. An additional factor in the
lower percentage of eligibility was intermittent work patterns to the
extent that an earlier study found that a higher percentage of
elderly Hispanic males (28%) were not social security insured, as
compared with only 7 percent of elderly whites (Garcia, 1980). In
the NHCoA study, if one assumes that the 12.3 percent of elderly
Hispanic males who were only receiving SSI (and "welfare"), but
not social security benefits, were not eligible for social security
benefits, this would suggest that one out of every eight elderly
Hispanic males were not social security eligible. One could
speculate that there has been an increase in the percentage of
elderly Hispanic males eligible for social security benefits due to
increasing job areas covered and higher entry into social security
covered employment.

It should be noted that an additional consideration in the low
level of benefit by elderly Hispanics was that a higher percentage of
that group chose actuarial reduced benefits; that is, they chose to
retire as early as age 62 (instead of age 65), thereby only drawing
as little as 80 percent of their benefits. Taking into consideration the
anticipated low benefit they were expected to receive at age 65, one
would ask why they would choose to receive reduced benefits as
low as 80 percent. If one accepts the limited data on life expectancy
of Hispanics and the more extensive data on the health status of this
group, it would appear that this group tended to choose early retirement not because they could afford to do so, but because their
health status was such that they were unable to remain in the labor
force. It should also be noted that the compounding effect of discrimination with that of age might have been a factor in the early

retirement decision of the elderly Hispanics who may not have been able to obtain jobs.

Size of Total Income

In 1984, the poverty rate for elderly Hispanics was twice that of all elderly, with the median income for elderly Hispanics being only 60 percent that of all elderly ($10,170.versus$6,040). This, in essence, reflects the economic status of Hispanics in later life with disproportionate dependence on social security and SSI and limited, if any, dependence on income from assets and private pensions.

Table 10
Total Income of All and Hispanic Elderly in 1984

Total Income	Aged Unites	
	All %	Hispanics %
Under $500	19	37
$50,000 or more	3	1
Median Income	$10,170	$6,040.

Source: Social Security Administration. Unpublished Data. 1987.

Availability and Utilization of Social Services

It is this author's contention that one of the factors that contributes to the non-utilization or under-utilization of existing services is a self-selecting-out process. Hispanics tend not to use services which they believe are for non-Hispanic whites or other groups. In addition, there is still a great deal of psychological scarring remaining, particularly for Mexican-Americans, due to mistreatment by the Immigration and Naturalization Service (INS) and other government agencies. (An example of this reaction to INS's past treatment of Hispanics is the unexpectedly low response to immigration reform legislation by illegal aliens residing in the United States).

In an earlier study, this author found a small, but significant, number of elderly Mexican-Americans who were social security insured but who were not receiving any social security benefit, it was suggested at that time that a number of factors may be at work, such as lack of knowledge on how to apply, lack of eligibility knowledge, language problems (as noted in findings of the NHCoA study), fear of authorities, and other reasons (Garcia, 1980).

Conclusions and Recommendations:

Over ten years ago this author began a major study of the economic status of Hispanic elderly using 1974 data from the U.S. Census Bureau, the Social Security Administration, and the Internal Revenue Service. The findings at that time were similar to those found in this study in regard to the economic status of elderly Hispanics as compared with that of elderly non-Hispanic whites. Perhaps the major finding of this current study is that the economic status of elderly Hispanics has improved slightly when compared with that of non-Hispanic elderly. But, that the economic status of non-elderly Hispanics has not improved, so that the economic status of the Hispanic elderly is better. There is much room for future research in this area which should include the nature of the changing relationship of Hispanic elderly to their families, taking into consideration the above findings. It is speculated that researchers will still find a certain level of familial intradependence, with the elderly Hispanic in a more stable financial situation.

Recommendations for Future Policy

Recommendations should include:

-- Variable retirement age for receipt of social security benefits taking into consideration the Latino population early entry into the workforce and earlier departure through illness, disability or death.

-- A greater complementarity between social security and SSI toward meeting some level of income adequacy for Hispanic elderly

-- A greater government involvement in developing and maintaining the intradependence of the Hispanic family.

There are several recommendations proposed that would apply to families that keep their elderly with them:

a. Tax credits

b. Personal tax deductions

c. Provisions against disincentives for keeping families together. For example, if both the family and the elderly person are on different programs of public assistance, efforts should be made against reducing either party's level of benefits due to their living in the same household. Family cohesion should be encouraged, not discouraged

The economic future of elderly Latinos remains a major concern. Only through a culturally sensitive analysis of existing policy and the development of culturally sensitive policy implementation will be to insure that future cohorts of elderly Hispanic are able to live their later years at a level of comfort they deserve.

PART IV:

Conclusions and Recommendations

Conclusions and Recommendations: Future Directions for the Development of Programs for the Hispanic Elderly

Herman Curiel and Marta Sotomayor

The works represented in this volume are based on a research project sponsored by the National Hispanic Council on Aging (NHCOA) and supported by the Administration on Aging, U.S. Department of Health & Human Services. The overall goal of the research effort was to identify individual and family interaction patterns that characterize coping styles that are associated with successful adaptation to aging amongst Hispanics. The contributors of this volume have examined various social, psychological, and environmental factors that influence elderly coping patterns in the context of the Hispanic intergenerational family.

There is consensus among the contributors that cultural factors must be taken into account in studying the aging process and in designing direct human services for Hispanic elderly. Hispanics are a heterogeneous population that are composed of a number of sub-groups (e.g. Mexican-American, Cuban, Puerto Rican, Central or South American) who share a common cultural and linguistic heritage that embodies an ethos that is viewed as foreign, not understood and/or accepted, by most policy makers and care providers. Frequently the effect is evident in underutilization rates of human service programs. This is so despite social-economic indicators like per capita income (less than two-thirds that of whites) and poverty rates (twice that of whites) plus evidence that elderly Hispanics are more likely than whites to suffer from chronic illness or disability and less likely to use long-term care services.

As a preface to presenting a synthesis of contributors' conclusions it is important to remind readers that this study was conducted in four Hispanic communities, one in Hartford, Connecticut, one in northern New Mexico and two in South Texas. Two of the latter are rural. Thus, there was an opportunity, in the same study and using the same instruments, to make comparisons at least between two Hispanic sub-groups. In each community two samples were identified, one an agency sample and the second a community sample. Sampling procedures were described earlier. A large pool of data was collected by NHCOA staff that included measures of self-esteem, mastery, activities of daily living, life satisfaction, health, religion and demographic information.

Researchers who had particular interests in the data collected were invited to analyze, interpret and share their findings in this form. Having multiple authors proved to be both a challenging and exciting experience for the authors and editors. Working independently, the authors sometimes expanded their original planned research focus so that some subjects overlap, as is evident in the preceding chapters. One positive result is that we have built-in means to double check our findings.

Another consequence of multiple users of the same data working independently is that the reported findings are not always consistent with others reported in the same volume. This can be anticipated when the same data is analyzed differently.

It is not possible to discuss in this concluding chapter all of the salient points made by the contributors, for they are many and substantive. We will attempt to synthesize the major points that have implications for policy makers and health and service care providers.

Growing old for the elderly represented in these four sub-populations was compounded by poverty, poor health conditions, discrimination, limited formal education, cultural alienation, language barriers and limited access to available resources. Despite these hardships, elderly in the four sites observed had better-than-average self-esteem. This is contrary to what might be expected given the identified high-stress indicators mentioned earlier. Equally puzzling were reported findings by González (p 31) on two sub-populations, South Texas (McAllen) and Puerto Rican (Hartford) who had the lowest incomes and the best psychological profiles with respect to mastery and self-esteem. Equally as interesting was a sense of religiosity, or "faith", that seemed to be shared by a great number of elderly study participants. It is quite possible that these findings provide a "glimpse" to that cultural ethos, that value system that has provided strength to our elderly to survive under such severe socio-economic barriers.

The family continues to be an important resource for Hispanic elderly, especially adult children. There are indications here that the extended family does not necessarily appear in its traditional format but is taking new forms where the elder lives separate from the nuclear family but continues to have frequent contacts via visits or telephone calls and assistance. As it is the case with the majority population, daughters play a significant role in the care-giving task.

The findings reported by Korte & Villa (p 65) on life satisfaction and its relationships to agency participation are note-worthy for program planners. Their findings indicate the female elder's participation in an agency program had a positive effect on life satisfaction. They did note that males across sites had lower agency participation, and with the one exception of South Texas, had lower life satisfaction scores.

Another noteworthy finding relates to the repeated indicators that suggest that the San Antonio elderly are a high psychological risk group. This is an unexpected finding given the size of the Hispanic population in that community and the level of resources that a community of that size can support. It was observed that these elderly were the most acculturated of the four subpopulations.

In conclusion, we are perplexed by a number of the findings. What is evident is that more research is needed to answer some of the questions that have been raised by the findings reported here. We concur with González's (p 33) observations that in truth the investigation of external factors that impact the Hispanic elderly's psychological well-being is at this time more theoretical than actual. Again, we echo his recommendation that future studies of psycholo-gical strength in Hispanic elderly must examine stress within the context of coping and the individuals' perception of their social reality.

Program recommendations:

We start by repeating what has been said by many other advocates for ethnic minority elderly groups. Program planners of human service programs need to build on features that complement the life experience or cultural norms of the consumer community. It is acknowledged that in some mixed ethnic communities this will be a challenging expectation. We believe that use of bilingual staff is a key ingredient in responding to the needs of this population group. At the very least, it is important that the agency receptionist be bilingual. Ideally, clients would have access to professional bilingual staff who are aware and sensitive to the many ramifications that this cultural reality implies. At the same time, we are quite aware of the diminishing pool of Hispanics who are finishing a four year college program and other advanced degrees that would give them the knowledge base and the practice skills to provide quality interventions to the elderly Hispanics and their families. Thus, bilingual bicultural services for Latino elderly cannot be discussed without addressing issues of training and education.

Other suggestions for creating a culturally sensitive agency climate include: use of signs in English and Spanish to designate floor directions, exits, public areas,and so forth. In addition, wall decorations that include paintings, furniture or sculpture that convey the message that the institutional representatives value the symbols of the ethnic elderly consumer.Of course, as evidenced in this study, Hispanics, like non-Hispanics, are not of one mind. There are rural and regional differences that influence expected norms.

We recommend that programs serving Hispanics use consumer advisory councils with members selected from the community or from an agency participant list. Such an advisory group can help staff identify consumer needs and ways to enhance the receptiveness of the agency program to the target community. We have noted that the configurations of the Hispanic family in relation to its elder members is changing. But then, this is to be expected for change does characterize modern society. The argument does not stop with acknowledging change, what is of most importance is the recognition that different family members shift roles according to need and circumstances throughout the life-span of individuals and families. Clusters composed of different family members form around certain problems, needs and issues allowing a pooling of personal and group resources that can be mobilized on behalf of the elderly family member.

In the future, more direct services for the elderly Hispanic will be required. As Korte notes, planners need to identify what are the key ingredients of a successful program that enhances life satisfaction. We need to also identify ways to increase elderly males' participation in agency programs, certainly by being more precise regarding their perception of services and what it means to them to ask for services.

We predict that future generations of elderly Hispanics will be more bilingual, bicultural, and will, like the San Antonio group, present more intrapsychic conflicts that will require additional mental health services. Existing theoretical frameworks that frame present interventions will need to be reviewed and in all probability revised to be applicable to this population group. It is only through efforts such as this that new conceptualizations will be formulated and new service delivery systems organized so that our elderly will receive the services they require.

Definitely more research is needed on the various and complex components of the life experience of the Hispanic elderly. In order to increase our knowledge base effectively, however, we will need to move away from doing isolated, one-time-only studies. We need a research agenda that is implemented over time with different sub-groups of Hispanic elderly to allow for comparisons and generalizations.

Bibliography

Adams, B. N. (1968). The middle-class adult and his widowed or still married mother. *Social Problems, 16*, 58-59.

Adams, D. L.(1969). Analysis of a life-satisfaction index. *Journal of Gerontology, 24* (4), 470-474.

Allport, G. (1960). *Religion in the developing personality.* Academy of Religion and Mental Health. New York: New York University Press.

American Heart Association (1984). *Heart facts.* The American Heart Association. Dallas, TX.

Andersen, R., Lewis, S.Z., Giachello, A.L., et al. (1981). Access to medical care among the Hispanic population of the southwest United States. *Journal of Health and Social Behaviors. 22* (1), 78-89.

Arlinger, R.L. (1982). Hypertension knowledge in a Hispanic community. *Nursing Research, 3* (4), 207-210.

Atchley, R. C. (1985). *Social forces and aging: An introduction to social gerontology.* (4th ed.) Belmont, CA.: Wadsworth Publishing.

Babbie, E. (1986). *The practice of social research,* (4th ed). Belmont, CA.: Wadsworth.Publishing

Baca-Zinn, M. (1979). Chicano family research: Conceptual distortions and alternative directions. *Journal of Ethnic Studies, 7,* 59-71.

Barrera, M. Jr., Zautra, A., & Baca, L.M. (1984). Some research considerations in studying stress and distress of Mexican-Americans. In J. Martinez, Jr. & R. H. Mendoza (Eds.), Chicano Psychology (pp. 223-247). New York: Academic Press.

Bastida, E. (1979). Family integration and adjustment to aging among Hispanic American elderly. Unpublished doctoral dissertation, University of Kansas.

Beaver, M. L. & Miller, D. (1985). *Clinical social work practice with the elderly: Primary, secondary, and tertiary prevention.* Chicago, IL: Dorsey Press.

Becerra, R.M., & Shaw, D. (1984). *The Hispanic elderly: A research reference guide.* Lanham, MD: University Press of America.

Bengtson, V. L. (1979). Ethnicity & aging: Problems in current social science inquiry. In Gelfand, D. E. & Kutzik, A. J. (Eds.). *Ethnicity & aging: Theory research & policy.* New York: Springer Publishing.

Berry, B. and Tischler, H. (1978). *Race & ethnic relations .* Boston, MA: Houghton Mifflin.

Blau, Z. S., Oser, G. T. & Stephens, R. C. (1979). Aging, social class, and ethnicity: A comparison of Anglo, Black, and Mexican-American Texans. *Pacific Sociological Review. 22* (4), 501-525.

Briggs, M. (1977). *The Chicano worker.* Austin, TX.: The University of Texas Press.

Brislin, R. W. (1970). Back-translation for cross-cultural research *Journal of Cross-Cultural Psychology ,1* (3), 185-216.

Brody, E.M. (1985). Parent care as a normative family stress. *The Gerontologist, 25* (1), 19-29.

Buriel, R., Calzada, S. & Vásquez, R. (1982). Relationship of traditional Mexican-American culture to adjustment and delinquency among three generations of Mexican-American male adolescents. *Hispanic Journal of Behavioral Science, 1 ,* 41-55.

Burnam, M.A., Telles, C. A., Karno, M., Hough, R. L. & Escober, J. I. (1987). Measurement of acculturation in a community population of Mexican-Americans. *Hispanic Journal of Behavioral Science, 2,* 105-130.

Burns, R. B. (1979). *The self-concept in theory, measurement, development and behavior.* New York: Longsman.

Cantor, M., and Mayer, M. (1976). Health and the inner-city elderly. *The Gerontologist, 16,* 19.

Cantor, M.H (1979). The informal support system of New York's inner city elderly: Is ethnicity a factor? In D.E. Gelfand and A.J. Kutzik (Eds.). *Ethnicity and aging: Theory research and policy.* (pp. 153-174). New York: Springer Publishing.

Cantor, M. H. (1983). Strain among caregivers: A study of experience in the United States. *The Gerontologist, 23,* 597-604.

Carp, F. M. & Carp, A. (1983). Structural stability of well-being factors across age and gender, and development of scales of well-being unbiased for age and gender. *Journal of Gerontology, 38,* 572-581.

Carrasquillo-Morales, H. A. (1983). Perceived social reciprocity and self-esteem among elderly barrio Antillean Hispanics and their familial informal networks. *Dissertation Abstracts International. 43* (7-A), 2463.

Castañeda, C. (1936-58). *Our catholic heritage in Texas.* (Vol. 5). Austin, TX: Von Boeckman-Jones.

Center on Budget and Policy Priorities (1986). Washington, D.C.: Government Printing Office.

Chan, K. B. (1977). Individual differences in reactions to stress and their personality and situational determinants: Some implications for community mental health. *Social Science Medicine, 11,* 89-103

Cicirelli, V.G. (1981). *Helping elderly parents: the role of adult children.* Boston: Auburn House.

Clark, M. (1959). *Health in the Mexican-American culture.* Berkeley, CA.: University of California.

Clark, M. & Anderson, B. G. (1967). *Culture and aging.* Springfield, Ill: Charles C. Thomas Publisher.

Clark, M. & Anderson, B. G. (1980). *Culture and aging: An anthropological study of older Americans.* New York: Arno Press.

Clark, M. & Mendelson, M. (1969). Mexican-American aged in San Francisco: A case description. *The Gerontologist, 9* (2), 90-95.

Cohen, J. (1968). Multiple regression as a general data-analytic system, *Psychological Bulletin, 20* (10), 426-433.

Colorado Interstate Research Associates (1974). *Summary of the 1974 Colorado state survey of minority elderly.* Denver, CO.

Cortés, C., Advisory Editor (1974). *Church views of the Mexican-American.* New York: Arno Press.

Croach, B. M. (1972). Aged and institutional support. Perceptions of older Mexican Americans. *Journal of Gerontology.,27,* 524-529.

Cromwell, R. E. & Ruiz, R. E. (1979). The myth of macho dominance In decision making within Mexican and Chicano families. *Hispanic Journal of Behavioral Science, 1,* 355-373.

Cubillos, H. L. (1987). *The Hispanic elderly: A demographic profile.* Washington, D.C.: National Council of La Raza.

Cuellar, J. B. (1978). El senior citizens' club. In M. B. Myerhoff & A. Simic (Eds.), *Life's career--Aging.* (pp.207-229). Beverly Hills, CA: Sage Publications,.

Cuellar, I., Harris, L.C., Jasso, R. (1980). An acculturation scale for Mexican-American normal and clinical populations. *Hispanic Journal of Behavioral Sciences, 2,* 199-217.

Dejong, G., Branch, L., & Corcoran, P. (1984). Independent living outcomes in spinal cord injury: Multivariate analysis. *Archives of Physical Medicine and Rehabilitation, 65,* 66-73

Development Associates, Inc. (1983). *Projections of the Hispanic population in the United States: 1990-2000.* Report submitted to the U.S. Department of Health and Human Services. Arlington, VA.

Díaz-Guerrero, R. (1955). Neurosis and the Mexican family structure. *American Journal of Psychiatry, 112,* 411-417.

Díaz-Guerrero, R. (1967). *Psychology of the Mexican: Culture and personality.* Austin, Texas: University of Texas Press.

Dowd, J. J., & Bengtson, V. L. (1978). Aging in minority populations: An examination of the double jeopardy hypothesis. *Journal of Gerontology, 33,* 427-436.

East Los Angeles Task Force (1975). Feasibility study to assess the health needs of the Spanish-speaking elderly in an urban setting. Unpublished manuscript, The Community Health Foundation. Los Angeles, CA.

Eisenstadt, S.N. (1974). Studies of modernization and sociological theory. *History and Theory 13.*(2), 225-52.

Feifel, H., Ed. (1959). *The meaning of death.* New York: McGraw-Hill.

Gann, L. H., & Duignan, P. J. (1986). *The Hispanics in the United States.* Boulder, CO: Westview Press.

García, A. (1980). The contribution of social security to the adequacy of income of elderly Chicanos. Unpublished doctoral dissertation. The Heller School, Brandeis University.

García, F., & de la Garza, R., (1977). *The Chicano political experience: Three perspectives.* North Scituate, Mass.: Duxbury Press.

García, J. A. (1982). Ethnicity and Chicanos: Measurement of ethnic identification, identity, and consciousness. *Hispanic Journal of Behavioral Science, 4,* 295-314.

Gelfand, D.E. (l982). *Aging: The ethnic factor.* Boston, MA.: Little, Brown.

George, L.K., & Bearon, L.B. (1980). *Quality of life in older persons.* New York: Human Sciences Press.

George, L. K. (1987). Self-esteem. In G. L. Maddox, Atchley, R. C., Poon, L. W., Roth, G. S., Siegler, I. C., Steinberg, R. M. & Corsini R. J. (Eds.). *The encyclopedia of aging.* New York: Springer Publishing.

Giachello, A.L., Bell, R., Aday, L.A., Andersen, R. (1980). Uses of the 1980 census for hispanic health services research. Paper presented at the meeting of the American Public Health Association. Detroit, MI.

Gibson, D. (1959). Protestantism in Latin American acculturation. Unpublished doctoral dissertation, University of Texas, Austin.

Glock, C. (1960). Religion and the integration of society. *Review of Religious Research, 2* (2), 49-61.

Gómez, E., Martin, H.W., Gibson, G. (1973). Adaptation of older Mexican-Americans: Some implications for social and health programs. Unpublished mimeo. Our Lady of the Lake University, San Antonio, TX.

Gómez, E., Martin, H.W., Gibson, G. (1976). Adaptations of older Mexican-Americans: Some implications for social and health progams. In *Emerging perspectives in Chicano mental health.* Houston, TX: Chicano Training Center.

González, J.R. (1982). Cognitive appraisal of stress events: A multi-method investigation. Unpublished doctoral dissertation, Arizona State University.

Grebler, L., Moore, J., and Guzmán, R. (1970). *The Mexican-American people, the nation's second largest minority .* New York: The Free Press.

Griffith, J. (1983). Relationship between acculturation and psychological impairment in adult Mexican-Americans. *Hispanic Journal of Behavioral Science, 5,* 431-460.

Griffith, J. & Villavicencio, S. (1985). Relationships among acculturation, socio-demographic characteristics and social supports in Mexican-American adults. *Hispanic Journal of Behavioral Sciences, 7,* 75-92.

Havighurst, R. J., Neugarten, B. L. & Tobin, S. (1963) Disengagement, personality and life satisfaction. In P. Hansen, (Ed.),.*Age with a future.* Copenhagen: Munksgaard.

Hays, W.C. and Mindel, C.H. (1973). Extended in relations in black and white families. *Journal of Marriage and the Family. 35,* 51-57.

Hazuda, H. P., Stern, M. P., et al., (1983). Ethnic differences in health knowledge and behaviors related to the prevention and treatment of coronary heart disease. *American Journal of Epidemiology, 117* (6), 717-728.

Hazuda, H. P. (1985). Differences in socio-economic status and acculturation among Mexican-Americans and risk for cardio-vascular disease. Unpublished manuscript, Task Force on Black and Minority Health. Department of Health and Human Services, Washington, D.C.

Hendricks J. and Hendricks Davis, D. (1986). *Aging in mass society.* Boston:, MA. Little, Brown.

Holahan C., & Holahan C. (1987). Self-efficacy, social support, and depression in aging: A longitudinal analysis. *Journal of Gerontology, 42,* 65-68.

Horowitz, A. (1982, May). *The role of families in providing long term care to the frail and chronically ill elderly living in the community.* Final report submitted to the Health Care Financing Administration, DHHS.

Hoyt, D. R., & Creech, J.C. (1983). The life satisfaction index: A methodological and theoretical critique, *Journal of Gerontology, 38* (1), 111- 116

Huyck, M. H. (1977). Sex, gender and aging. *Humanitas, 13.*

Israel, B. A. and Antonucci, T.C. (1987). Social network characteristics and psychological well-being: A replication and extension. *Health Education Quarterly. 14,* 461-481.

Jackson, J. J. (1970). Aged Negroes: Their cultural departures from statistical stereotypes and rural-urban differences. *The Gerontologist, 10,* 140-145.

Jackson, J.J. (1978). Special health problems of aged blacks. *Aging,* 287-288, 15-20.

Jaco, E.G. (1957). Social factors in mental disorders in Texas. *Social Problems, 4,* 322-328.

Juárez, R.Z. (l983). Lower Rio Grande Valley: l983 elderly needs assessment survey. Edinburg, TX: Pan American University, Center for Aging.

Juárez, R.Z. (1984). Health status of Mexican-American and Anglo elderly in South Texas. Paper presented at the Annual Meeting of the American Public Health Association, Anaheim, CA.

Karno, M. (1966). The enigma of ethnicity in a psychiatric clinic. *Archives of General Psychiatry, 14* (5), 516-520.

Karno, M. & Edgerton, R. B. (1969). Perceptions of mental illness in a Mexican-American community. *Archives of General Psychiatry, 20* (1), 233-238.

Kauffman, C., Randolph, S.M., Drake, V.D., and Gelfand, D. (1987). *Characteristics and needs of black caregivers and their elderly clients in personal care homes.* Final report submitted to the Administration on Aging, DHHS. February. American National Red Cross, Washington, D.C.

Keef, S.E., Padilla, A.M., and Carlos, M. L. (1978). The Mexican-American extended family as an emotional support system. In J. M. Casas and S.E. Keef (Eds.), *Family and mental health in the Mexican-American community.* Los Angeles, CA; The Spanish Speaking Mental Health Research Center.

Kerlinger, F.N. & Pedhazur, E.J. (1973). *Multiple regression in behavioral research.* New York, Holt, Reinhart and Winston.

Kessler, R. C., & Cleary, P. D. (1980). Social class and psychological distress. *American Sociological Review, 45* , 463-478.

Kessler, R.C., Price, R.H., and Wortman, C.B. (1985).Social factors in psychopathology: Stress social support, and coping processes. In M.R. Rosenzweig & L.W. Porter (Eds.), *Annual Review of Psychology, 36* Palo Alto, CA: Annual Reviews, Inc.

Kluckholn, F., and Strodbeck, F. (1961). *Variations in values orientations.* IL: Row, Peterson.

Korman, A. (1971). Environmental ambiguity and locus of control as inter-active influences in satisfaction. *Journal of Applied Psychology, 55* , 399-402.

Korte, A. O. (1978). Social interaction and morale of Spanish-speaking elderly. Unpublished doctoral dissertation, University of Denver, Denver, CO.

Korte, A.O. (1982). Social interaction and morale of Spanish-speaking rural and urban elderly. *Journal of Gerontological Social Work 4* (3/4), 57-66.

Korte, A. O. (1983). Theoretical perspectives in mental health & the Mexicano elders. In M. Miranda & R. A. Ruiz (Eds.). *Chicano aging and mental health,* (pp. 1-37). Washington, D.C.: U.S. Department of Health & Human Services, NIMH, p.21.

Korte, A.O. (1983). La mortificación: An interactional view. In G. Gibson (Ed.), *Our kingdom stands on brittle glass* National Association of Social Workers.

Kosberg, J. (1980). Family maltreatment: causality and practice issues. Paper presented at the 33rd Annual Meeting of the Gerontological Society of America, San Diego, CA.

Krause, N. (I986). Social support, stress, and well-being among older adults. *Journal of Gerontology, 4I,* 5I2-5I9.

Krause, N. (I986). Stress and coping: Reconceptualizing the role of locus of control beliefs. *Journal of Gerontology, 4I,* 6I7-622.

Krause, N. I987). Stress in racial differences in self-reported health among the elderly. *Gerontological Society of America, 27,* 72-76.

Lacayo, C.G. (1980). *A national study to assess the service needs of the Hispanic elderly: Final report.*.Asociacion Nacional Pro Personas Mayores, Los Angeles, CA.

LaRocco, J., French, J., Jr., & House, J. (1980). Social support, occupational stress, and health. *Journal of Health and Social Behavior, 21* 202-218.

Larsen, R. (1978) Thirty years of research on the subjective well-being of older americans. *Journal of Gerontology, 33* (1), 109-125.

Laurel, N. (1976). An intergenerational comparision of attitudes toward the support of aged parents: A study of Mexican-Americans in two South Texas communities. Unpublished doctoral dissertation. University of Southern California.

Lazarus, R.S., Averill, J.R., & Opton, E.M. Jr. (I974). The psychology of coping: Issues of research and assessment. In G.V. Coehlo, D.A. Hamburg, & J.E. Adams (Eds.), *Coping and adaptation.* (pp. 249-29I). New York: Basic Books.

Leonard, O. E. (1967). The older rural Spanish people of the Southwest. In E. G. Youman's (Ed.), *Older Rural Americans.* Lexington: University of Kentucky Press.

Liang, J. (1984). Dimensions of the life satisfaction index A: A structural formulation. *Journal of Gerontology, 39* (5), 613-622.

Liang, J., Tran, T. V., & Markides K. S. (1988). Differences in the structure of life satisfaction index in three generations of Mexican-Americans. *Journal of Gerontology, 43* (1), S1-S8.

Linn, M. W., Hunter, K. I. & Perry, P. R. (1979). Differences by sex and ethnicity in the psychosocial adjustment of the elderly. *Journal of Health and social behavior, 20* (3), 273-281.

Litwak, E. (1965). Extended kin relations in an industrial democratic society. In E. Shanas and G. Streib (Eds.), *Social structures and the family: Generational relations* (pp. 290-326). Englewood Cliffs, N.J. Prentice Hall.

Lohr, J., Esses, J.M, & Klein, M.H. (1988). The relationship of coping responses to physical health staus and life satisfaction among older women. *Journal of Gerontology: Psychological sciences. 43* (2), 54-60.

López-Aqueres, W. (1985). An assessment of the rehabilitation, physical and mental health status of the elderly Hispanic: Highlights of findings. Unplublished manuscript . University of Southern California, Rehabilitation Research and Training Center on Aging, Rancho Los Amigos Hospital, Los Angeles, CA.

Lowenthal, M.F. (1964). *Lives in distress.* New York: Basic Books.

Lowenthal, M., Thurner, M., & Chiriboga, D. (1975). *Four stages of life* San Francisco: Jossey-Bass.

Maldonado, D. (1975). The Chicano aged. *Social Work, 20* (3), 213-216.

Maldonado, D. Jr. (l985). The Hispanic Elderly: A socio historical framework for public policy. *Journal of Applied Gerontology,4,* 6-17.

Maldonado, D. (1985). A historical framework for understanding the Hispanic elderly. In D. Maldonado and E. Applewhite (Eds.) *Cross-cultural social work practice in aging: A Hispanic perspective.* Arlington, TX: University of Texas at Arlington.

Maldonado-Sierra, E. D., Fernández, R. M. & Trent, R. D. (1958). Three basic themes in Mexican and Puerto Rican family values. *Journal of Social Psychology, 48,* 167-181.

Markides, K.S., & Martin, H. (1979). A causal model of life satisfaction among the elderly. *Journal of Gerontology, 34,* 86-93.

Markides, K. S. (1980). Correlates of life satisfaction among older Mexican-Americans and Anglos. *Journal of Minority Aging,* 5 (2), 183-190.

Markides, K.S. (1981). Letter to the editor. *Journal of Gerontology, 36,* 494.

Markides, K.S. (1983). Minority aging. In M.W. Riley, B.B. Hess, & K. Bond (Eds.), *Aging in society: Selected reviews of recent research.* Hillsdale, NJ.: Lawrence Erlbaum.

Markides, K.S., Martin, H.W.& Gómez, E. (1983). Older Mexican-Americans: A study in an urban barrio. Unpublished manuscript. The University of Texas Center for Mexican-American Studies, Austin, TX.

Markides, K.S., Martin, H.W.& Gómez,E.(1983). *Older Mexican-Americans: A study in an urban barrio.* The Mexican-American Monograph Series, Center for Mexican-American Studies. Austin, TX.: The University of Texas Press.

Markides, K.S., Boldt, J., & Ray, L. (1986). Source of helping and intergenerational solidarity. A three-generations study of Mexican-Americans. *Journal of Gerontology, 41,* 506-511.

Markides, K. S. & Mindel, C. H. (1987). *Aging & ethnicity.* Newbury Park, CA: Sage Publications.

Martínez, M. (1981). The Mexican-American family: A weakened support system? In E.P. Stanford (Ed.), *Proceedings of the seventh national institute on minority aging* (pp. 145-151). San Diego, California: University Center on Aging, College of Human Services, San Diego State University.

McNeely, R. L. & Colen, J. L. (1983). *Aging in minority groups.* Beverly Hills, CA: Sage Publications.

Meinhart, K. & Vega, W. (1982). Health and social correlates of mental health. Unpublished manuscript.

Mena, F. J., Padilla, A. M. & Maldonado, M. (1987). Acculturative stress and specific coping strategies among immigrant and later generation college students. *Hispanic Journal of Behavioral Science, 4,* 207-225.

Mendoza, A. P. (1981). Responding to stress: Ethnic and sex differences in coping behavior. In A. Baron, Jr. (Ed.), *Explorations in Chicano psychology* (pp. 187-212). New York: Praeger.

Miller, D. C. (1983). *Handbook of Research Design and Social Measurement* (4th ed). New York: Longman.

Miranda, M. R., & Ruiz, R. A. (1981). *Chicano aging and mental health.* Washington, D.C.: U.S. Superintendent of Documents.

Miranda, M. R. (1984). Mental health and the Chicano elderly. In J. Martinez, Jr. & R. H. Mendoza (Eds.), *Chicano psychology* (pp. 207-221). New York: Academic Press.

Montiel, M. (1978). Chicanos in the United States: An overview of socio-historical context and emerging perspectives. In M. Montiel (Ed.), *Hispanic families.* Washington, D.C.:National Coaliton of Hispanic Mental Health and Human Service Organizations.

Moustafa, A.T., Weiss, G. (1968). Health status and practices of Mexican-Americans. Mexican-American Study Project, Advance Report II. Graduate School of Business Administration. Los Angeles: University of California.

Mutran, E. (1986). Family support among blacks and whites: Response to culture or socio-economic differences. In L.E. Troll (Ed.), *Family Issues in Current Gerontology.* New York: Springer.

Myers, R.S. (1980). Self-help groups: An overview. In R. Wright (Ed.), *Black/Chicano elderly: Service delivery within a cultural context. Proceedings of the First Annual Symposium on the Black/Chicano elderly..* Arlington, TX: The University of Texas at Arlington.

National Council of Churches in the U.S.A., Bureau of Research and Survey, Series A-E. *Churches and church membership in the United States: An enumeration and analysis by countries, states , and regions.* New York: National Council of Churches, 1956-1958.

National Hispanic Council on Aging (1986). *The National Hispanic Council on Aging Final Report* (AoA Grant Number: 90AR0056) Washington, D.C.: National Hispanic Council on Aging.

Neugarten, B.L., Havighurst, R.J., & Tobin, S.S. (1961). The measurement of life satisfaction. *Journal of Gerontology, 16* (2), 134-143.

Newton, F. Cota-Robles. (1980). Issues in research and service delivery among Mexican-American elderly: A concise statement with recommendations. *The Gerontologist, 20* (2), 208-213.

Newton, F. Cota-Robles. & Ruíz, R. A. (1981). Chicano culture and mental health among the elderly. In M. Miranda & R. A. Ruíz (Eds.), *Chicago aging and mental health* (pp. 38-75). Washington, D.C.: U.S. Department of Health and Human Services.

Nie, N.H., Hull, C.H., Jenkins, J.G., Steinbrenner, K.& Bent, D.H. (1975). *SPSS: Statistical package for the social sciences* . New York: McGraw-Hill

Nuñez, F. (1975, October). Variation in fulfillment of expectations of social interaction and morale among aging Mexican-Americans and Anglos. University of Southern California. Paper presented at The Gerontological Society Meeting, Louisville.

OARS Older American Resource and Services Schedule (1975). Durham, NC.: Duke University Center for the Study of Aging and Human Development.

Ortegón, S. (1950). Religious thought and practice among Mexican Baptists in the United States. Unpublished doctoral dissertation, University of Southern California.

Osberg, J., Corcoran, P., Dejong, G., & Ostroff, E. (1983). Environmental barriers and the neurologically impaired patient. *Seminars in Neurology, 3,* 180-194.

Osberg, J., Dejong, G., McGinnis, G., & Seward, M. (1987). Life-satisfaction and quality of life among disabled elderly adults. *Journal of Gerontology, 42,* 228-230.

Padilla , A. M. & Aranda , P. (1974). Latino Mental Health: Bibliography and Abstracts. Washington, D.C.,: U.S.Government Printing Office.

Padilla, A. M., & Ruíz, R. A. (1974). *Latino mental health: A review of the literature.* Rockville, Maryland: National Institute of Mental Health.

Pearlin, L. I., & Schooler, C. (1978). The structure of coping. *Journal of Health and Social Behavior 19* (3), 2-21.

Perlin, L., Menaghan, E. G. , Liberman, M. A., & Mullan, J.T. (1981). The stress process. *Journal of Health and Social Behavior, 22,* 337-356.

Ramírez, A.E., Herrick, K.L. and Weaver, F.J. (1981, summer). El asesino silencioso: A methodology for alerting the Spanish-speaking community. *Urban Health: The Journal of Health Care in the Cities.* 44-48.

Ramos, R. (l979). Movidas: The methodological and theoretical relevance of interractional strategies. In N.K. Denzin (Ed.), *Studies in Symbolic interaction.* Greenwich, CT: JAI Press.

Rankin, M. (1975). *Twenty years among the Mexicans: A narrative of missionary labor.* Cincinnati, OH: Chase and Hall .

Roberts, R.E. & Lee, E.S. (1980). The health of Mexican-Americans: Evidence from the human population laboratory studies. *American Journal of Public Health. 70,* 375-384.

Robinson, J.P. & Shaver, P.R. (1973). *Measures of social psychological attitudes* (rev. ed.). Ann Arbor, MI.: Survey Research Center, Institute for Social Research, The University of Michigan.

Romano, O. I. (1960). Donship in a Mexican-American community in Texas. *American Anthropologist, 62,* 966-976.

Rosenberg, Morris (1965). *Society and the adolescent self-image.* Princeton: Princeton University Press.

Rubel, A. J. (1966). *Across the tracks: Mexican-Americans in a Texas city.* Austin, TX.: The University of Texas Press.

Sanchez-Mayers, M. (1985). Hispanic cultural resources for prevention and self-help. In D. Maldonado & E. Applewhite (Eds.), *Cross-cultural social work practice in aging: A Hispanic perspective.* Arlington, TX: The University of Texas at Arlington.

Schaefer, R. (1984). *Racial and ethnic groups* (2nd ed.).Boston, MA.: Little, Brown.

Schulz, J. (1976). *The economics of aging .* Belmont, CA: Wadsworth Publishing.

Shanas, E. (1967). Family help patterns and social class in three countries. *Journal of Marriage and the Family, 27,* 257-266.

Shanas, E. (1979). The family as a social support system in old age. *The Gerontologist. 19,* 169-174.

Shanas, E., & Maddox, G. (1985). Health, health resoures, and the utilization of care. In R.H. Binstock & E. Shanas (Eds.), *Handbook of aging and the social sciences* (2nd ed.). New York: Van Nostrand Reinhold.

Shanas, E.(1986). The family as a social support system in old age. In L.E. Troll (Ed.), *Family issues in current gerontology.* New York: Springer.

Simic, A. (1985). Ethnicity as a resource for the aged: An anthropological perspective. *Journal of Applied Gerontology, 4,* 65-71.

Simmons, L. (1960). Aging in pre-industrial societies. In C.Tibbits (Ed.) *Handbook of social gerontology* (pp.62-91). Chicago, IL.: University of Chicago Press.

Smith, W. D., Burlew, A. K., Mosley, M. H., & Whitney, W. M. (1978). *Minority issues in mental health.* Reading, Mass.: Addison-Wesley.

Sotomayor, M. (1973). A study of Chicano grandparents in an urban barrio. Unpublished doctoral dissertation, School of Social Work, University of Denver, Denver, CO.

Spitzer, A. (1960). Religious structure in Mexico. *Alpha Kappa Delta.*

Stern, M. P., Pugh, J.A., Gaskill, S.P. (1982). Knowledge, attitudes, and behavior related to obesity and dieting in Mexican-Americans and Anglos: the San Antonio Heart Study. *American Journal of Epidemiology. 115* (6). 917-927.

Streib, G.F. (1978). Family patterns in retirement. *Journal of Social Issues. 14*, 46-60.

Sussman, M.B. (1959). The isolated nuclear family: Fact or fiction? *Social Problems. 6*, 330-340.

Sussman, M. & Burchinal, L. (1962). Kin family network: Unheralded structure in current conceptualization of family functioning. *Marriage and Family Living, 24*, 231-240.

Szapocznik, J. & Kurtines, W. (1980). Acculturation, biculturalism and adjustment among Cuban Americans. In. A. M. Padilla (ED.), *Acculturation: Theory, models, and some new findings* (pp. 139-159). Boulder, CO: Westview Press.

Szapocznik, J., Kurtines, W. M. & Fernandez, T. (1980). Bicultural involvement and adjustment in Hispanic American youths. *International Journal of Intercultural Relations, 4,* 353-365.

Texas Statewide Health Coordinating Council (1982). *The Texas State Health Plan 1982-1986.* Austin, TX.

Thotis, P.A. (1983). Dimensions of life events that influence psychological distress: An evaluation and synthesis of the literature. In H.B. Kaplan (Ed), *Psychological stress: Trends in theory and research.* New York: Academic Press.

Torres-Gil, F. (1978). Age, health and culture: An examination of health among Spanish-speaking elderly. In M. Montiel (Ed.), *Hispanic Families.* Washington, D.C.: Natural Coalition of Hispanic Mental Health and Human Services Organizations.

Treviño, F.M. (1982). Editorial: Vital and health statistics for the U.S. Hispanic population. *American Journal of Public Health. 72* (9), 979-981.

Treviño, F., Moss, A.J. (1983). Health insurance coverage and physician visits among Hispanic and non-Hispanic people. In *Health-United States, 1983.* (pp.45-48). DHHS Publication Number (PHS) 84-1231. Public Health Service. Washington, D.C.: U.S. Government Printing Office.

Troll, L.E. (1971). The family of later life: A decade review. *Journal of Marriage and the Family. 33*, 263-290.

U.S. Census (1985). *Persons of Spanish origin in the United States,*
  March 1982. P. 20, No. 396. Washington. D.C.: U.S.Government
  Printing Office.
U.S. Department of Commerce. Bureau of Census (1987).
U.S. Department of Commerce. Bureau of the Census. (1981, May)
  1980 census of population: Supplementary reports. .
  Washington, D.C.: U.S. Government Printing Office.
U.S. Department of Commerce. Bureau of the Census. (1981).
  Persons of Spanish origin in the United States: March 1980.
  Advance report) . *Current population reports.* Series 20,
  No. 351. Washington, D.C.: U.S. Government Printing Office.
U.S. Department of Commerce, Bureau of the Census (1983).
  Conditions of Hispanics in America today. Washington, D.C.:
  U.S. Government Printing Office.
U. S. Department of Commerce, Bureau of the Census. (July,
  1984).*Census, ethnic and Spanish statistics: Selected social and
  economic characteristics of the population by sex and birth of
  Spanish origin.* Washington, D.C.: U.S. Government Printing
  Office.
U.S. Department of Commerce. Bureau of the Census .(September,
  1987). *Special Population Reports.* Washington, D.C.:
  U.S.Government Printing Office.
U.S. Department of Health and Human Services. (1980). *Health of the
  disadvantaged: Chart book 11.* Public Health Service, DHHS
  Publication No. (HRA) 85-2209. Washington, D.C.: U.S.
  Government Printing Office.
U.S. Department of Health and Human Services. (August, 1985)
  Report of the Secretary's task force on Black and Minority health.
  Executive Summary, Volume I. Washington, D.C.: U.S.Govern-
  ment Printing Office.
U.S. Department of Health and Human Services (January,1986).
  Report of the Secretary's task force on Black and Minority health.
  Volume VIII: Hispanic Health Issues. Washington, D.C.: U.S.
  Government Printing Office.
U.S. Department of Health and Human Services. (1985). *Utilization of
  hospital in-patient services by elderly Americans.* National Center
  for Health Services Research and Health Care Technology
  Assessment. DHHS Publication No. (PHS) 85-3351.
  Washington, D.C.: U.S. Government Printing Office.
U.S. Department of Health and Human Services.(July, 1984)
  National Center for Health Statistics. *Births of Hispanic
  parentage. 33* (8).Supplement. Washington, D.C.: U.S.
  Government Printing Office.
Valle, R., & Martínez, C. (1981). Natural networks of elderly
  Latinos of Mexican heritage: Implications for mental health. In

M. Miranda & R.A. Ruiz (Eds.), *Chicano aging and mental health*. Rockville, MD: National Institute of Mental Health.

Valle, R., & Mendoza, L. (1978). *The elderly Latino*. San Diego, CA: Center on Aging, California State University at San Diego.

Varghese, R., & Medinger, F. (1979). Fatalism in response to stress among the minority aged. In D. E. Gelfand & A. J. Kuzik (Eds.), *Ethnicity and aging: Theory, research and policy* (pp. 96-115). New York: Springer.

Vega, W. (1980). Defining Hispanic high-risk groups: Targeting populations for health promotion. In R. Valle & W. Vega (Eds.) *Hispanic Natural Support Systems*. Sacramento: State of California Department of Mental Health.

Vernon, G. M. (1962). *Sociology of religion*. New York: McGraw Hill.

Ward R. A. (1983) The stability of racial differences across age strata: An assessment of double jeopardy. *Sociology and Social Research, 67*, 312-323.

Weiss, J. (1971). Effects of coping behavior with and without a feedback signal on stress pathology in rats. *Journal of Comparative and Physiological Psychology, 77,* 22-30.

Wilder, A. & Niven, I. (1958). *Theology and modern literature*. Cambridge, MA: Harvard University.

Wood V., Wylie M. L. & Schaefer B. (1969). An analysis of a short self-report measure of life-satisfaction: Correlation with rater judgments. *Journal of Gerontology, 24,* 465-469.

Wright, R. Saleebey, D., Watts, T., & Lecca, P. (1983). *Transcultural perspectives in the human services: Organizational issues and trends*. Springfield, IL: Charles C. Thomas

Wrinkle, R., Garza, R., & Polinard, J. (April, 1987). Ties that bind? Gender, ethnicity and political attitudes: A comparison of Anglo and Mexican-American women. Paper presented at the meeting of the Midwest Political Science Association, Chicago, IL.

Wylie, M. L. (1970). Life satisfaction as a program impact criterion. *Journal of Gerontology, 25* (1), 36-40.

Wyle, F. M. (1971). Attitudes toward aging and the aged among black Americans: Some historical perspectives. *Aging and Human Development. 2,* 66-70.

Zopf, Paul E., Jr. (1986). *America's older population*. Houston,TX.: Cap and Gown Press.

Zúñiga-Martínez, M. (1979). Los ancianos: A study of the attitudes of Mexican-Americans regarding support of the elderly. Unpublished doctoral disseration. Brandeis Univerity, Waltham, Mass.

Zúñiga-Martínez, M. (Summer, 1979). Family policy for Mexican-Americans and their aged. *The urban and social change review. 12* (2).

Contributors

Anzaldua, Hermila, MSW, Associate Professor,
Department of Sociology & Social Work,
Pan American University, Edinburg, Texas.

Bastida, Elena, Ph.D., Associate Professor,
Department of Sociology & Social Work,
Wichita State University, Wichita, Kansas.

Curiel, Herman, Ph.D., Assistant Professor,
School of Social Work,
University of Oklahoma, Norman, Oklahoma.

Gallego, Daniel T. , Ph.D., Professor and Director,
Center on Aging,
Webster State College, Ogden, Utah.

García, Alejandro, Ph.D., Professor,
School of Social Work,
Syracuse University, Syracuse, New York.

Gibson, Guadalupe, MSW, Professor Emeritus,
Worden School of Social Service,
Our Lady of the Lake University, San Antonio, Texas.

Gonzalez, Genaro, Ph.D., Assistant Professor,
Department of Psychology,
Pan American University, Edinburg, Texas.

Korte, Alvin, Ph.D., Professor,
Social Work Department,
New Mexico Highlands University, Las Vegas, New Mexico.

Randolph, Suzanne, Ph.D., Assistant Professor,
Depart.of Family & Community Development,
University of Maryland, College Park, Maryland.

Reed-Sanders, Delores, Ph.D., Associate Professor,
    Department of Sociology,
    Pan American University, Edinburg, Texas.

Rosenthal, James A., Ph.D., Assistant Professor,
    School of Social Work,
    University of Oklahoma, Norman, Oklahoma.

Sotomayor, Marta, Ph.D., President,
    National Hispanic Council on Aging,
    Washington, D.C.

Villa, Roberto F., MSW,
    Department of Social Work,
    New Mexico Highlands University, Las Vegas, New Mexico.

Wrinkle, Robert D., Ph.D., Professor,
    Department of Political Science,
    Pan American University, Edinburg, Texas.